RUSSO-POLISH RELATIONS

First published January 1945
by the Cresset Press Ltd 11 Fitzroy Square London W1
printed by The Shenval Press, London and Hertford

RUSSO-POLISH
RELATIONS

AN HISTORICAL SURVEY

Edited by

S. KONOVALOV

Professor of Russian in the University of Birmingham
Lecturer in Slavonic Studies at the University of Oxford

LONDON

THE CRESSET PRESS

1945

CONTENTS

INTRODUCTORY NOTE

THE PRESENT SURVEY is based on Sir John Maynard's report undertaken at the invitation of the Anglo-Soviet Public Relations Association (*President:* Lord Horder; *Chairman of Executive:* Miss Eleanor Rathbone, M.P.). Sir John's death in December 1943 prevented him from completing it for submission to the Association.

I have been asked: (1) to prepare for publication such parts of Sir John's MS. as had clearly been given final form and were not debarred from inclusion by subsequent pronouncements and events, and (2) to supplement these passages with additional and connective material, bringing the account of events up to the spring of 1944.

Anxious to safeguard Sir John's presentation of the subject, I have confined myself almost exclusively to the use of documents and authoritative statements. Yet it is hardly fitting to issue this survey in its present form over the name of Sir John Maynard, since 18 sections (out of 36) have been added by me, as also 7 Appendices and 6 Maps.

Sir John is the author of sections 2, 3, 5, 6, 11, 12, 26 and 33; and sections 1, 8, 14–18, 20–22 embody material cited by him from Professor B. H. Sumner's *Survey of Russian History*. From the same book I was kindly allowed by the author to borrow additional matter for sections 4, 7, 13, 19, 23, and one Map (No. I). To these I have added another thirteen supplementary paragraphs, of which two (30 and 31) make considerable use of material prepared by Sir John.

Our gratitude is due to Lady Maynard, Professor B. H. Sumner and his publishers (Messrs. Duckworth) for kind permission to make use of the material, without which this report could not have appeared in its present form. We are also glad to acknowledge our special indebtedness for kind permission to quote: to *The Times*, the Royal Institute for International Affairs and to Mr. C. Smogorzewski.

S. Konovalov

HISTORICAL SURVEY

1

FOR THE LAST six hundred years the three major facts in the history of the Slavs have been the Ottoman conquest, the German expansion and power, and the conflicts, military, religious, and cultural, dividing the Russians and the Poles. Until the eighteenth century the other Slavs meant for the Russians almost solely the Poles, who were their only immediate neighbours. For both Russia and Poland, their long and deep estrangement has been hitherto of greater weight than any of the various ties linking the Slav peoples together.

Since July 1941 Russians and Poles have been fighting in the common cause against Hitlerite Germany. Never before in history has it happened that *all* Russians and *all* Poles have been joined in a struggle against a common foe. "Certainly", as a Soviet writer has put it (1941), "it was not easy to bridge the gulf which for ages divided Russians and Poles", but "the Russian people have a deep respect for sorrow and still more for courage". May this feeling, with its consequences, be reciprocated by both peoples!

2

The main elements in the picture up to 1600 are the following:

(*a*) The choice, at the time of Christianisation in the tenth century, by Russia of the Orthodox Church of Byzantium, by the Poles of the Church of Rome, which turned the eyes of the one to the East, and of the other to the West, and set a barrier between the two.

(*b*) The occupation in 1340 of the fortress town of Lvov by the Poles, and its fortification as a basis of defence against Tatar and Turkish invasion.

(*c*) The incorporation, between 1250 and 1450, of Western Russia (White Russia and northern Ukraine) in the Grand Duchy of Lithuania, partly through conquest, partly through other means.

(*d*) The union of the Grand Duchy of Lithuania with the Kingdom of Poland in 1385–6. The acceptance of Catholicism by the Lithuanians and the gradual polonization of the upper classes, the culture, and the institutions of the Grand Duchy.

(*e*) The creation in 1596 of the Greek Catholic or Uniat Church, which was meant to be a bridge between the Western and Eastern Communions and to bring as many Orthodox believers as possible under the jurisdiction of Rome.

3

In regard to paragraph (*b*) in the preceding section, the occupation of Lvov by Casimir the Great: a veritable No-Man's Land had come into existence between the rivers San and Dnieper. This happened when the oldest Russia, that of Kiev and the adjoining principalities, was destroyed by the Mongols in the thirteenth century, and the line of the Dukes of Halicz (Galicia) subsequently became extinct. It came to be known as *Ukraina*, the Borderland, and was for three centuries a battle-ground between the Christian West and the Moham-medans. The fortification of Lvov was an assertion by the Polish Crown of a claim to this borderland and an undertaking to defend it against Turks and Tatars. It enjoyed alternate periods of relative peace and bitter wars under leaders, mostly of the higher nobility, who held vast estates from the Polish Crown. Attracted by the fertility of the soil and the milder climate, a steady stream of colonists filtered in from the west, peasants, artisans and tradesmen. The indigenous population retained for two hundred years its Orthodox faith and its own speech and pattern of living. This indigenous element in the so-called Western Lands—Western, viewed from the stand-point of the newer Russia—remained a link between the Russia of Kiev and the Russia of Moscow. The pattern of life was, of course, that of the nobles with their retainers and peasants, more or less in a condition of serfdom. Very soon, however, the upper classes tended to be assimilated to western culture, many of the gentry became polonized, and from the sixteenth century onwards the demands made on their peasantry were so tightened up as to provoke class reactions, leading to the violent revolt led by Khmelnitsky in 1648.

Much of the attractive force of this more developed western civilization was due to the zealous activities of the Roman Church, more especially after the coming of the Jesuit Fathers to Poland in 1565; and the creation of the Uniat Church a generation later was on their initiative.

4

It has already been emphasised that one major consequence of the Mongol invasion was the complete disruption of Kiev Russia. The principalities between the Oka and the Volga and, to the north, Novgorod and Pskov developed along their own lines in vassalage to the Golden Horde. The Russian principalities of the upper Dnieper and westwards, including Kiev itself, harried by and paying frequent tribute to the Tatars, slowly coalesced into the loosely knit Grand Duchy of Lithuania. The rich Galician principality, likewise Russian, after a period of independent brilliance in the thirteenth century, sank into being an apple of discord between Lithuania, Poland, and Hungary, and after 1350 fell to Poland.

Thus, between 1250 and 1450, before Muscovy became consolidated, Lithuania rose to be the major Russian State. By 1450 she stretched from the Baltic about Memel to the Black Sea, very insecurely at the mouths of the Dniester and the Dnieper; from the Bug on the west, eastwards well beyond the Dnieper and Smolensk and Kiev. She was within a hundred miles of Moscow and doing her best to prevent the growth of Muscovy; she was pressing hard upon Novgorod and expanding to the upper Oka and into the wooded steppe beyond the Dnieper.

This was a joint Lithuanian-Russian achievement; for except in the north, where the Lithuanian tribes formed a solid bloc, the Grand Duchy was peopled by Russians, developing into White Russians and Ukrainians.

5

The original partnership of Poland and Lithuania was dictated largely by the threat to both countries of the German Knights of the Cross, operating from East Prussia. As things turned out, and for good reasons, Poland (the Crown Land), became the dominant partner, and not a few Lithuanian nobles were restive as a result. But the essential point to be grasped here is *what was meant* by Lithuania. In the late 1200s and the early 1300s this tiny warrior people living close to the Baltic shores had been invited by their White Russian neighbours to the south and south east to come to their help in fighting the Tatars. The result was an extension of heathen Lithuanian control over the vast plainland (one might compare the conquests of the Northmen by sea in western Europe) whose population was not Lithuanian and pagan, but *White Russian and Orthodox*. No settled administration was possible under these circumstances, and yet all this world was nominally included in the new Joint Kingdom. In joining Poland, Lithuania allowed the Ukrainian lands to be treated as part of the Crown Land, while White Russia remained part of Lithuania.

6

These newly attached areas offered an inviting field for cultural activities, in particular for the missionaries of the Western church. The Lithuanians, following the example of their Grand Duke, accepted the Roman faith; and the White Russians, nominally Orthodox, tended also to come under the influence of Western Christianity. What is more, just as in the south so too here, the upper classes were attracted to the more developed cultural pattern of living of the west, including the advantages of association with the Royal Court; with the result that the whole of the Lithuanian nobility became Polish —although not always to the extent claimed by Polish historians, and not to the extent of sacrificing their regional rights and ambitions. Finally, under the leadership of the Jesuit Fathers, every town community became the seat of a church educational centre, the work of which was soon to make itself felt in both private and public living.

From the point of view of political consolidation this was all to the good, and it justifies in part the habit that in time grew up of calling the whole Joint Kingdom by the name 'Poland', a designation which has no historical justification. This process of assimilation, however, stopped with the upper classes. In no part of these huge eastern *Kresy* (Borderlands) were the non-Polish speaking masses (chiefly peasants) ever brought into this process. Large areas did indeed become Roman Catholic, still larger areas (chiefly in the south) came into the Uniat Church; but they kept their own speech, they remained almost illiterate, and they were conscious of the social and economic inferiority under which they laboured as against the ruling classes. Not only then were they not assimilated to Polish culture, but numbers of Polish colonists (Catholic in faith) who settled in these new lands, were assimilated to their milieu and ceased to be Poles.

7

The 'Western Lands' and Eastern Galicia were, and always had been non-Polish in the sense that, taken as a whole, the great majority of the inhabitants were Ukrainian and White Russian or Lithuanian. Except for Eastern Galicia they had formed, since the fourteenth century, part of the Grand Duchy of Lithuania, which itself was more and more closely linked with the Kingdom of Poland, since 1386 through a common dynasty, since 1569 (the Union of Lublin) in a species of federated union. Thus the great Poland of the fifteenth to the eighteenth century was (like the Muscovite Empire) a composite state, with the western half Polish, the eastern half Russian or Lithuanian. . . .

From the fifteenth to the seventeenth century the disputed lands were even larger than those described in Section 4, extending far to the Dvina and the Dnieper. For these three centuries Muscovy stood against Lithuania and Poland in almost continual struggle, for one century unsuccessfully, for the next successfully, for the last again unsuccessfully, until (1654–67) the tide turned definitely in her favour.

8

At the beginning of the seventeenth century Muscovy was submerged in social strife, civil war, and Polish and Swedish intervention, culminating in the occupation of Moscow and Novgorod and the instalment of a Polish Tsar. This was the Time of Troubles (1604–13).

It was long before Russia forgot the part played by the Poles in the disintegration of Muscovy, in the period of weakness when the Crown was left vacant by the extinction of the line of Ivan the Terrible. At that time Sigismund III of Poland, on the crest of the Counter-Reformation, moved forward with an eastern policy that might ultimately have achieved another and even greater union than that of Poland with Lithuania. First one pretender Polish Tsar, then a second, each with the same Polish wife, were set up with Polish armed support; great stretches of Muscovy were occupied or over-run; Smolensk was captured, after a twenty-one months' siege; twice the Poles seized Moscow itself. Finally Sigismund's son and heir, Vladislav, was installed there as Tsar, with the help of one section of the Muscovite magnates (1610–12). He was eventually driven out by the wave of national resistance organised by

Minin and Pozharsky from the Vŏlga and Northern Districts, and young Michael Romanov was elected Tsar (1613). This period of Polish ascendancy and humiliation for Moscow left the bitterest memories, and the names of Minin and Pozharsky have been honoured by Russians ever since, as the symbol of the patriotic rallying against "our enemies and outragers of the Christian faith, the Polish and Lithuanian men".

Though Moscow had been regained and the Polish Tsar evicted, Muscovy was too weak to reconquer Smolensk and other territory lost to the Poles, and on the north-west to the Swedes. She had been thrust back to where she was before 1500.

9

During the reign of Sigismund III the Polish Empire had become the most spacious in Europe, comprising with vassal lands 1,075,000 sq. km. "In 1618 the territory of the Joint Kingdom (Poland and Lithuania) was almost equal to that of Germany and France taken together." (Professor Stanislaw Kot.)

"About 1580 the population of Poland proper was from 4 to 4½ million, and together with the Southern Ruthenian territories nearly seven million, while with Prussia, Lithuania and Livonia it amounted to about ten million. By the middle of the seventeenth century the population had grown to thirteen or fourteen million". (Professor F. Bujak.) The population of Russia reached thirteen million only three quarters of a century later, in 1725.

10

It was not until 1634 that Vladislav renounced the Russian crown and recognised Michael Romanov as the Tsar of Russia.

"The Tsardom of the Romanov dynasty in 1613 followed days in which at least the partition of Muscovy seemed imminent. . . . The Polish eastern frontier lay close to Pskov and

13

embraced the vital fortress of Smolensk together with Kiev, the Jerusalem of the Russian race. Southern Poland included the Carpathians, and through its Dnieper region gained contact with the Black Sea. . . . The peace of Andrussov (1667) transferred to the Tsar a broad belt of White Russia, comprising Smolensk, Chernigov, Kiev and Poltava, and inevitably suggesting further advances along lines of race, geography and religion." (*The Cambridge History of Poland* 1697–1935, [1941], pp. xiii–xiv.)

[See Appendix No. 1, and Map No. I.]

11

At the middle of the 1600s, Bohdan Khmelnitsky, who himself had had a Polish education, was able to rally the disaffected elements in the whole Dnieper region and launch a revolt against those who ruled them, calling in the Tatars and even the Turks to help him in a war that threatened the very existence of the Polish Commonwealth. What is more, when he was unable to get the terms he demanded, he could turn to the now rising power of Moscow in the north for help, and on the plea of Orthodox kinship enlist the support of 'The Third Rome', the Patriarchate of the East, in a war of religion against an 'aggressive' Catholic Poland. The upshot was a ceding of part of the Ukraine to Russia, and increased interest by Moscow in the rest of this region.

Intervention of this kind would have had less chance of success had the Catholic hierarchy been willing to accord real equality to its non-Catholic neighbours in the Polish-Lithuanian Commonwealth. As it was, the Roman bishops resisted every effort of their Orthodox colleagues to secure seats in the Senate—and in the main they were successful. Further, although many of the Catholic nobility were generous in providing funds for the building of Orthodox places of worship, the general tendency was in the opposite direction. Finally, many of the Lithuanian nobility who went over to the Protes-

MAP I. Reproduced from *A Survey of Russian History* by Professor B. H. Sumner

tant faith landed in the bosom of Catholicism. In general the non-Catholic elements came more and more to feel that at best they were treated as 'poor relations'.

12

"From 1648 it became clear that Poland was threatened with catastrophe and disorder. A nation that had been strong and flourishing slipped into poverty and disorder, from which it never really recovered till the disaster of the Partitions. . . . Between 1600 and 1700 Poland had only fifteen years without a war, while Britain had seventy-five". (*Five Centuries of Polish Learning* by Professor Stanislaw Kot, Basil Blackwell, Oxford, 1941, pp. 11–12.)

John Sobiesky, the hero of Vienna (died 1696) was the last Polish King to represent the choice of the Polish people. The next two sovereigns were Germans from Dresden, and the third—coming to the throne in 1764—although a Pole, was the nominee and one-time favourite of the Empress Catherine. It was a calamity for Poland that it had no real leadership during the first three-quarters of the eighteenth century—the years in which Prussia was "starving her way to greatness" as a kingdom, and Russia, first under the genius of Peter the Great and then under the resolute ambition of Catherine, was rising to be one of the first Powers in Europe. Peter, after a fierce struggle, triumphed over Charles XII of Sweden at Poltava in 1709. Poland had been a passive spectator, and from that year her lands were never to be free from the presence of Russian agents and Russian military units. Peter had plans for acquiring parts of the Joint Kingdom, but they were to be realised only later, beginning from the First Partition in 1772.

13

The Russian share in the First Partition of 1772 was the north-eastern corner of the 'Western Lands', almost wholly

White Russian, relatively poor, but strategically and commercially important for Russia since she now secured the whole eastern bank of the Dnieper and the northern bank of the Dvina, so that Riga, Russian since 1721, was linked directly with Smolensk. (See Map No. I.) The eventual annexation of this region had been approved by Catherine ten years earlier in secret conclave with her counsellors, and the usual view that in this First Partition she was duped by Frederick is incorrect, though she may have had her hand forced.

The Polish element in the region was very weak, and taken by itself the loss to Poland was not serious and its acquisition by Russia could be justified. But what was extremely serious was that its acquisition, unlike the gains of 1667, was the result of a deal between the three eastern powers. Henceforward the solution of the question of the 'Western Lands' in a sense favourable to Russia was tied up with Prussian and Austrian designs, which unlike the Russian had little or no religious, national, or historic backing. It was no longer an inter-Slav problem, but a catspaw of European diplomacy.

Twenty years later, in the Second and Third partitions (1793 and 1795), the whole of the 'Western Lands' fell to Russia, while Prussia and Austria divided the remainder of Poland. [See Appendix No. 2 and Map No. I.]

14

The three partitions gave to Russia the whole of the long-disputed 'Western Lands', the old Grand Duchy of Lithuania, with over 6,000,000 new subjects. The western frontier, after the further acquisition of the mainly Polish district of Bialystok in 1807, was almost exactly the same as the new Soviet frontier in the autumn of 1939, apart from Eastern Galicia. Except for the Polish or polonized upper class and the Catholic and Uniat clergy, the eastern part of these lands was almost solidly White Russian, the southern Ukrainian, both of them mixed Orthodox and Uniat: efforts to raise them in the final struggle for independence, or later, had hardly any success. In the western part the Poles were more numerous, especially in Vilna, and Polish influence was deeper. In the northern part illiterate Catholic Lithuanian peasants predominated. On the whole, if the question of the 'Western Lands' could have been separated from that of partition, the Russian gains in the first and second partitions were justifiable, those in the third much less so.

15

For the main mass of the people the Russian annexation for some time made little difference, save in two respects: Orthodoxy had full scope, and there were better conditions for the towns. In these Russia for the first time came in contact with the Jewish problem on a large scale and with anti-Semitism, which, with its strong economic roots, was already locally virulent, though a century later it was deliberately intensified by the worst elements in reactionary tsarism. Serfdom remained as before; very onerous, though perhaps less arbitrary than in the rest of the Empire. Law and custom likewise remained substantially as before. The Catholics were tolerated, and the Jesuits even favoured. The Polish upper-class minority, in addition to the actual fighting, suffered in many cases individually from repressive measures, but most of them kept their land and the large grants made to Russian nobles were made chiefly at the expense of the state and church land. The Poles of course ceased to be the rulers of the country, but they retained much of their position in local government, except in the region acquired in the First Partition which was handed over to Russian officials and rapidly assimilated to the rest of the Empire.

Apart from this region the great bulk of what was acquired in the other two partitions was governed during the reigns of Paul (1796–1801) and Alexander I (1801–25) under a special regime, which, especially under the latter, reflected his friendly attitude towards the Poles. The local administration was mostly in the hands of Poles, and a special army, 'the Lithuanian Corps', was created, which was linked with Warsaw, not St. Petersburg. Czartoryski, scion of one of the greatest of the Polish noble families, the confidant and early foreign minister of Alexander, was allowed to build up at Vilna a university which for twenty years (1803–23) was the centre of education and Polish culture for the 'Western Lands', and in fact nourished a new generation on the aspirations of Polish nationalism.

This last was the cardinal fact. The Polish state had been extinguished in 1795, but not Polish national feeling. Hitherto Russia and Poland had been divided by two different civilizations and by disputed territory; now there was added a third cause of division, loss of independence; after 1815 a fourth, inclusion of the majority of Poles in Russia, and after 1830 their subjection to Russian oppression.

16

The Polish question, as much as the Continental System and even more than the Turkish question, caused Napoleon's 1812 campaign, which was a reply to a projected campaign of Alexander through the Grand Duchy in the previous year. Napoleon himself began by calling 1812 'the second Polish war'. As soon as it opened the Diet in Warsaw proclaimed the restoration of Poland and summoned the 'Western Lands' to rise; 1812 was to be a war of national reconquest. The summons was none too successful; but in the Grand Duchy there were 85,000 Poles, and none excelled them in enthusiasm and bravery.

Three years later Napoleon was in St. Helena and Poland was for the fourth time partitioned, after a long and almost violent tussle between the powers at the Congress of Vienna. Posen, Thorn and Danzig returned to Prussia, while the rest of the Grand Duchy went to Alexander as his 'Polish Kingdom', in official style, unofficially known as 'Congress Poland'. (See Map No. II.) Austria remained in possession of Galicia, except

MAP II. Congress Kingdom of Poland

for Cracow, which was erected into a tiny free state, until Nicholas I insisted that an end be made of this "hotbed of a vast new conspiracy whose ramifications embrace all the former Polish provinces", and it was accordingly annexed to Austria in 1846.

17

In 1815 for the first time Russia was joined with the core of Poland, the central Vistula lands centred on Warsaw with some 3,000,000 Poles (and two or three hundred thousand Jews). This 'Congress Poland' was originally entirely distinct from the Empire, with a separate crown hereditary in the house of

20

Romanov. Like the Grand Duchy of Finland, conquered by Alexander from Sweden in 1809, his 'Polish Kingdom' had a constitution of its own, drawn up in 1815 by Poles on moderate liberal lines (except as regards the Jews), which gave them a parliament, full internal self-government with separate finance and tariffs, and an army—"a snake spouting its venom at us", as a Russian official protested. Under this regime the Poles organized considerable economic prosperity for fifteen years. But the constitution was not adhered to by the Russians. They felt—and they were right—that the 'Polish Kingdom' would be used as a stepping-stone to the incorporation in it of the 'Western Lands'. The Poles had fought for that in 1794 and 1812, and they were to fight for it again in 1830 and 1863.

18

Russians distinguished sharply between the 'Western Lands' and 'Congress Poland'. The former, as not being Polish, must never return to Poland and must be governed quite differently from it. As regards 'Congress Poland' opinion differed. Many would have preferred that Russia should have stayed on her frontiers when Napoleon had been driven out in 1812, and should have left the Grand Duchy to its fate and washed her hands of the Poles. This solution was later wistfully contemplated from time to time even in the very highest quarters. It had two great defects: after 1815 it meant abdication on the part of the Tsar as Polish king, an almost impossible step; and it meant also the almost certain aggrandizement of Prussia and probably Austria, and incalculable international complications.

To most Russians the constitutional regime given to 'Congress Poland' not only opened the way to most dangerous influences in the 'Western Lands', but was incompatible with the position of the Tsar in the rest of his dominions. Most, though not all, Russians were not prepared for a transformation of tsarism into some kind of constitutional monarchy along Western lines; nor for that matter was Alexander himself. The rising tide of conservative nationalism, which found full expression under Nicholas I, was already by 1815 very strong where Poland was concerned. The only antidote to the anti-Polish chauvinism current in most sections of Russian society that counted for anything, could have been a growing liberal movement in Russia. But this sole support for his Polish policy Alexander no longer encouraged. In his own way as much an autocrat as his father Paul, he was sympathetic towards liberal reforms only in so far as he himself granted them; and they must be gratefully received without criticism. The last of the enlightened despots, and therefore fundamentally at odds with the spirit of liberalism, he substantially agreed with Madame de Staël when she said to him: "Your soul is the best constitution for your people." At home, and in Poland, he swung more and more to the right, "wrapt in some moral fog", and his closing years (1820–25) seemed as "the darkness of a prolonged eclipse".

19

The 1830 rising was not merely a revolt of the upper- and middle-class nationalists, but, unlike the guerilla struggle of 1863, a full-scale war owing to the existence of a well-trained Polish army and the Lithuanian Corps. The Russians, however, were bound to win in the end unless assistance was forthcoming from abroad. None came. Polish hopes of French aid, as always, were far too sanguine.

While the Polish revolt prevented any effective intervention by Nicholas I in the settlement of the Belgian revolution, that crisis equally prevented any effective intervention on behalf of Poland. As in the case of Napoleon III's diplomatic campaign against Russia in the 1863 revolt, French and British sympathy with the Polish cause merely intensified Russian national feeling against the Poles and 'the calumniators of Russia', presuming to intervene in 'this contest of Slavs with Slavs, this ancient domestic contest', that did not concern and could not be understood by Europe. England in particular had better remember Ireland.

Nevertheless, between 1830 and 1863, the Polish question was a stormy petrel of European international relations, and the Polish *émigrés* and their quasi-government in Paris were a perpetual preoccupation for Nicholas. In any case, even apart from the West, the Polish question could not be a purely internal problem simply owing to the existence of a Prussian and an Austrian Poland. In 1830 the three eastern powers, and in 1863 Russia and Prussia, though not yet Austria, marched literally hand in hand.

The Russian reaction in 1830 was to treat 'Congress Poland' as a conquered country, though still distinct from the rest of the Empire. The 1815 constitution was swept away and until the death of Nicholas in 1855 the Russian hand lay heavier and heavier upon the country. In the 'Western Lands' full assimilation with the rest of the Empire was henceforward the order of the day: a long series of anti-Polish measures was introduced and a powerful campaign launched against the Uniat Church.

20

The internal crisis in Russia during the early years of Alexander II had its effect on policy towards 'Congress Poland'. Under the Polish nobleman Wielopolski, a number of reforms were made which gave some scope to Polish development, and there seemed a chance of an understanding between Polish and Russian conservative adherents of moderate reform. It proved impossible. The blunders of the government incited the nationalist societies to rebellion. They declared Alexander deposed and an independent Poland with the 'Western Lands'.

Alexander (and Russia was behind him) refused to return even to 1815, for he feared that it would be but a stepping-

stone to 1772. "There can be no question especially of a constitution or a national army", he wrote just before the revolt,
in private instructions to his brother, the Viceroy of Poland,
"I will allow neither the one nor the other in any form. To
agree to them would be to abdicate from Poland and recognize
its independence with all its baneful consequences for Russia,
namely her deprival of all that was in the past conquered by
Poland which Polish patriots continue to regard as belonging
to them".

The rebellion of 1863 was crushed in blood, and the Russian
reaction to it was even more severe than in 1830. Everything
that was regarded as tainted with 'polonism', i.e. the identifying
of the Polish people with "the armed propaganda of Latinism
in the midst of the Slav world", was systematically attacked.
There was ruthless repression by an administration that was
now, as it had not hitherto been, almost purely Russian in
personnel. The extreme was reached when Russian was
required to be taught even in village schools and religious
teaching in Polish was prohibited. At the same time Russian
policy in certain respects deliberately favoured the peasantry
and industrial development as a means of countering 'polonism'.

21

The Polish cause was weakened by social and political divisions among the Poles themselves, both at home and in the
émigré camp, divisions that had been accentuated by the effect
of the French Revolution. Above all there was the fact that
most of the Poles in 'Congress Poland' were a backward
peasantry, thirty to forty per cent of them landless in the
middle of the nineteenth century, in technical methods and
general standards not much above the Russian peasantry.
The Napoleonic edict of liberation of 1807 and earlier attempts
at peasant reform had led in practice to little change in the
rule of the Polish landowning class.

This failure gave the Russians the opportunity to adopt a land reform policy, from 1846 onwards, which aimed at representing the Russian Tsar as the friend of the Polish peasant, in opposition to the Polish landowner. The peasantry took little part in the 1830 rebellion and on the whole a secondary part in 1863, though the revolutionary government did then, in contrast with 1830, make far-reaching promises to them. As an offset to these and a pendant to the emancipation of the serfs in Russia, the Russian government enacted a land law (1864) in 'Congress Poland' directed against the Polish landowners, whereby the peasantry received about four times as much land as the Russian in the central Russian lands and under very much easier conditions.

The small, but growing, Polish professional and small bourgeois class supplied, together with the lesser gentry, the driving force of the 1863 rebellion, whereas in that of 1830 they had been subordinate to the nobility and bigger landowners. After 1863, again in contrast with 1830, there was no large emigration, and the Polish (and Jewish) urban working class and professional middle class increased steadily with the industrial development (mainly textiles and coal) of 'Congress Poland'. This was favoured by the abolition in 1851 of the customs frontier between it and Russia and the consequent opening of the large Russian market to Polish manufactures. At the same time there was a wide opening in Russia for Polish skill in railway building, engineering, and other professions. All this was the economic basis for the post-1863 generation of so-called 'organic work' or 'Warsaw positivism' in contrast with the previous generation of militant nationalism and messianic romanticism typified by the great triad of *émigrés* patriot poets, Mickiewicz, Krasinski, and Slowacki.

22

By 1900 resigned caution and economic betterment no longer sufficed for the younger generation, but both the National

Democratic Party, which grew up under the leadership of Dmowski, and the much smaller and divided socialist groups were strongly influenced, in different ways, by the change in the economic structure of Poland and its very close economic ties with Russia. Further, the increasingly anti-Polish policy of Germany in her Polish lands, especially in the form of their colonization by Germans (a policy never attempted by Russia in her compactly Polish lands), encouraged Dmowski and many Poles to choose as the lesser evil temporary collaboration against the common enemy with Russia, where it was hoped that the liberal and revolutionary movements might extract from the government concessions to Poland.

23

The outbreak of war in 1914 found the Poles necessarily divided. The response of the Russian Poles was far more favourable than might have been expected, in part thanks to the moving proclamation issued under the signature of the commander-in-chief, the Grand Duke Nicholas. But reactionary Russian nationalism remained the dominant influence with the Tsar, and, despite discreet pressure from France and Great Britain, nothing of any value could be extracted from him in favour of Poland. On the other hand, though both the liberal and the revolutionary parties in Russia were prepared to recognize the freedom of ethnographic Poland (as they did after the Revolution of March 1917), they did not interpret this as including any large part of the 'Western Lands'.

24

Nor did the aspirations of important sections of Polish opinion in Russia go, at that time, far beyond the claim of an independent Poland within ethnographic confines. The Russian liberals and socialists, who were sympathetic to the Polish cause, were certainly under the impression that their interpretation of future Polish frontiers was, on the whole, shared by the Poles. The following quotation, from an article which appeared early in the autumn of 1914 in a Polish weekly review *Kraj*, may illustrate this. This influential Polish review, founded in Russia in 1882, was edited by Erasme Piltz, who later, together with Roman Dmowski, presented the Polish claims to the Paris Peace Conference (on 29 January 1919).

"Only Russian nationalistic circles, and Ukrainian and Lithuanian chauvinists, considered that we had any desire to rule over foreign territories. The Poles have long ago given up such dreams—at least those of them who are capable of intelligent thought. . . .

"From 1863 onwards, that is, for more than fifty years, we have been realizing that our political possessions, by the nature of things, must necessarily be limited to real Polish lands. And at the present moment there cannot be two views on this subject. Among all our political parties there is not one which interprets the Jagellonian idea* as our 'friends' represent it. We have no claims on Lithuania or on any other Russian territory in the sense of striving for domination there. In this respect we are unanimous in principle. Even members of the National Democratic Party, more frequently than all others accused of trying to create a Poland 'od morza do morza' (from

---

*[The period of the Jagellon dynasty (1386–1572) was the age in which Poland rose to the position of premier power in Europe as regards both population and territory. The Jagellonian Empire arose through the marriage of the Lithuanian ruler Jagailo (Jagello) to the Polish Queen Jadwiga in 1386. Lithuania, which then included parts of White Russia and the Ukraine, remained till 1569 a distinct principality often under a Grand Duke of its own, who, however, was always a member of the dynasty. In 1569 the Union of Lublin consolidated and integrated the two states and the Western Russian Lands passed into the category of Lands of the Polish Crown, with the exception of White Russia which remained directly attached to Lithuania. At the height of its power, the Polish-Lithuanian State stretched from the Baltic to the Black Sea ('od morza do morza'—'from sea to sea'), including besides the Western Russian Lands, some parts of Prussia and Courland, and extending various degrees of hegemony and political influence over Livonia, Estonia, Moldavia, Vallachia and Bessarabia. The dream of this Jagellonian Empire remained a lodestar of leading Polish politicians when Poland was eclipsed in her turn. On Pilsudski's Jagellonian programme, see Appendix No. 5, (c), p. 67.—EDITOR'S NOTE.]

MAP III. Reproduced from *La Question Polonaise* by Roman Dmowski; Armand Colin, Paris, 1909. (Names have been translated from French.) *Ref. p.* 31

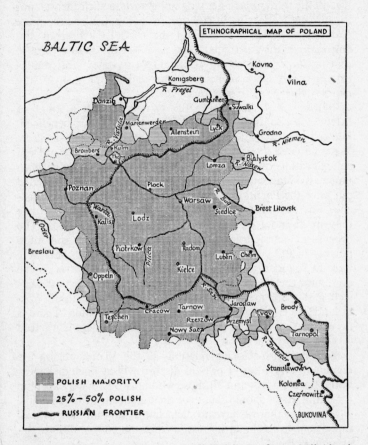

MAP IV. Based upon the map published in Professor Milyukov's newspaper *Rech* (Autumn 1914). Reproduced here from *Voina i Polsha*, Moscow, 1914. (Names have been translated from Russian)

Ref. p. 31

the Baltic to the Black Sea), do not entertain such ideas,—not to speak of those political groups going farther than the National Democratic Party on the road to liberalism and national equality of rights. They have not the slightest doubt that in border regions our political role has inevitably diminished, from the time when in these regions the mass of the people achieved self-consciousness. . . .

"History has shown that the extreme Polish attempt to extend the country's influence was not at the time beneficial, but only harmed the life and solidarity of the Polish State. We conquered too much—and this very fact prevented us from concentrating on our own country, which would have been more advantageous for us. The political experiments, carried out after the Partitions, convinced us that the stubborn insistence on the Polish character of Lithuania and the Ukraine only made more difficult our relationships with Russia. The process of democratization which advanced more and more quickly in the borderlands-finally made it evident that there was no foundation for the maintenance of the Poles as the dominating element there. All this we now understand very well and there are no dreamers among us who think of a Poland extending as far as Smolensk, or even Vilna. There is no need to sober us in this connection just as there is no need to give us any warnings. . . .

"When Polish-Russian relations in the Vistula region are regulated, all causes of present discord will at once disappear in the borderlands, and all those who now obstinately keep on repeating 'Poles should renounce their claims to Russian lands' —will realise that we have no such claims and that our political aspirations are voluntarily restricted to the confines of ethnographic Poland."

(*Voina i Polsha*. The Polish Question in the Russian and Polish Press. Collection of articles by Prof. A. Kizevetter, L. Kozlowski, A. Lednicki, L. Krzywicki, Prof. P. Milyukov, A. Swentohowski and others. With ethnographical map of Poland. [Our Map No. IV.] Moscow, 1914. Pp. 81–83, & 87.)

On 8 July 1915 Roman Dmowski, Leader of the National Democratic Party (later first Polish delegate at the Paris Peace Conference and signatory of the Treaty of Versailles), when speaking to the 'Russian State Commission on the Polish Question' declared that *the Poles did not consider as Polish the ancient eastern regions of Poland (Kresy).* *

If we compare Maps Nos. III and IV, we are struck at once by the fact that at the time (1909–1914) the Polish and the Russian conception of ethnographical Poland envisaged a similar configuration. An English map of racial boundaries in Europe (not reproduced here) published in the *Round Table* and in 8 editions (1914–16) of *The War and Democracy* (by Seton-Watson, Dover Wilson, Alfred Zimmern and Arthur Greenwood), agrees with Maps Nos. III and IV. The ethnographical line there follows the future Curzon Line very closely, running, however, somewhat further to the west in its southern sector.

25

While the Polish political parties in Russia placed their faith in the Allied cause (which meant a loyal attitude towards Russia), the Poles under Austria and Germany showed a different political orientation. "At the outbreak of the war all Polish parties in Galicia, without distinction of political aspiration, declared that the Poles in Galicia would fulfil to the end

*Roman Dmowski declared on behalf of the Polish representatives: "As far as the South- and North-Eastern regions are concerned, it must be borne in mind that, at the present time, after the spread of culture among the masses of the people which went on in the nineteenth century, the question of the national character of the region must be decided not by the language of the educated and well-to-do minority but by the language of the mass of the people. And, therefore, the Poles who in the first half of the last century held Lithuania, Volhynia, Podolia and the Ukraine to be Polish lands, now . . . no longer consider Lithuanian and Russian lands to be Polish, and on the Polish side the inclusion of these lands within the boundaries of Poland is not suggested. . . . When at present politicians speak of Poland, they mean ethnographic Poland." (Quoted from Professor Szymon Askenazy, *Uwagi*. Warszawa. 1924. p. 440.)

their obligations towards their Monarch, considering that their national honour demanded it, so that nobody could reproach them with ingratitude." (Professor S. Grabski's secret Memorandum to the Russian Government, 1915. Published in *Polsko-Russkie Otnoshenia*. Tsentrarkhiv, Moscow, 1926, p. 29.) The attitude of Pilsudski could be summed up in the saying attributed to him in the summer of 1914: "The Polish question will be decided in our favour if Germany is victorious against Russia, but is herself defeated by France".

* * *

"Pilsudski and his group of national revolutionaries started on the side of the Central Powers, but renounced nothing; and through a most extraordinary combination of events their dreams came true. All the three partitioning Powers collapsed, and Poland re-arose in a void. It seemed no longer necessary 'to weigh interests and measure distances'. But while the incredible can be achieved at a juncture, can it be made to last? Pilsudski planned to break up Russia, and to recreate a 'Jagellon' Union with an 'independent' Ukraine and White-Russia (and also with Lithuania). The scheme was impracticable: anti-Russian separatism was almost non-existent outside East Galicia; moreover, a deep social gulf divided the peasantries of the borderlands from the Poles".

('Russia and Poland', Special Article, *The Times*, 14 January 1944.)

26

The Russian Revolution broke out in March 1917. To the Russian Provisional Government of Prince Lvov belongs the credit of the first pronouncement in regard to Polish independence: "Poles! The old political system of Russia, source of our common bondage and our disunity, is now overthrown for ever. Free Russia . . . hastens to send you her fraternal greeting; she calls you to a new life, to freedom. . . . The Russian nation, having won its freedom, concedes to its brother

Polish nation the full right to determine its own life as it wishes. . . . The Provisional Government will assist in the forming of an Independent Polish State, *composed of all territories where Poles are in a majority*, as a pledge of enduring peace in a newly organized Europe". This declaration freed the hands of the Allies in the west, with the consequences known to all.

In the autumn of 1918, as a sequel tó the revolutionary programme, the Soviet authorities published a decree annulling "all treaties and agreements concluded between the government of the former Russian Empire and the governments of the Kingdom of Prussia and of the Austro-Hungarian Empire concerning the Partitions of Poland". To this statement the Poles attach great value, taking it to mean an end of the plan for the dismembering of their ancient homeland.

27

"The thirteenth of President Wilson's points postulated 'an independent Polish State . . . which should include the territories inhabited by indisputably Polish populations'; and by Article 87 of the Treaty of Versailles Poland agreed that her boundaries not laid down in that treaty shall be 'subsequently determined by the Principal Allied and Associated Powers'. These frontiers were the subject of careful study and of discussion in which the Polish case was fully stated and considered, whereas Russia was without official representation or direct influence. The only counterweight to the very active pressure exerted by the Poles was the thought about a more distant future, when Russia would have recovered; this was present especially in the minds of the British delegation.

"On 21 April 1919, the Commission on Polish Affairs reported on the northern sector of Poland's eastern frontier, down to about Kholm, agreement on that province being delayed by British doubts concerning its eastern, predominantly Ukrainian, districts. Eventually, however, the whole province was assigned to Poland, with the River Bug for frontier. The northern sector of the frontier was then approved on 8 December 1919, in a declaration of the Supreme Council, signed by Clemenceau as president. The southern sector was fixed in the East Galician Statute, adopted on 20 November 1919 but cancelled a month later in deference to Polish opposition, which turned the French; still, the allied views on what was indisputably Polish territory in Galicia were re-stated in the 'Certain Frontiers' Treaty of 10 August 1920. [For further particulars on the question of Eastern Galicia see Appendix No. 3.]

"In July, 1920, after the defeat of the Polish expedition against Kiev, the Bolsheviks gained a temporary ascendancy and the Poles had to seek allied protection: a chance now seemed to open of establishing the frontier previously sanctioned by the Supreme Council. With Polish consent it was proposed to Soviet Russia by Lord Curzon (and thus became associated with his name) as an armistice line to which the Polish forces were to retire pending a peace conference to be held in London. But this was not a mere demarcation line suggested by momentary considerations: the intention was that the 'provisional' should endure." ('Russia and Poland', Special Article, *The Times*, 14 January 1944.)

28

In Appendix No. 4, we give extracts from the now famous Curzon Note of 11 July 1920.

The proposal, though made with the approval of the Polish Prime Minister, could not be popular in Poland, especially as the seriousness of the military situation was not yet fully realized by the Polish public. In the words of *Gazeta Poranna* (Warsaw, 17 July 1920) it meant the end of "the illusion that Poland could settle the Russian question without Western Europe".

In Soviet Russia at the time when the Red Army—after long

months of retreat—was advancing into Poland, with the prospect of reaching Warsaw, the Curzon proposal was received with extreme suspicion. Mr. Chicherin, in his reply of 18 July —to the 'ultimatum' as he calls the note—says that he would "meet the wishes and interests of the Polish people the more fully, the more the Polish people in its internal life enter upon the path of creating a solid basis for really fraternal relations between the labouring masses of Poland, Russia, the Ukraine, White Russia and Lithuania"; insists on "guarantees that Poland will cease to be an instrument of aggression and intrigue"; considers "with some caution such proposals so far as they do not come directly from the Government concerned and so long as the danger subsists that the attitude of the Polish Government will not correspond to the declarations of other Governments which speak in its name", since "numerous utterances of representatives of the Polish people have come to the knowledge of the Soviet Government in which they express themselves in an extremely bitter sense as to the British Government's political action on this question"; points out that "the past attitude of the British Government in the conflict . . . can hardly be considered as a reason for assuming the role of mediator"; "absolutely rejects the claims of any group of Powers to assume the role of supreme masters of the fate of other nations"; expresses the willingness of the Soviet Government "to agree to a territorial frontier more favourable to the Polish people than the frontiers indicated by the Supreme Council in December 1919" and its desire to start "direct negotiations with Poland".

* * *

". . . The Bolsheviks failed to reach Warsaw; soon the tide turned, and the Poles regained complete superiority. They rejected pleas for self-determination for Lithuania, White Russia, and the Ukraine and a proposal for a plebiscite in East Galicia. At Riga they dictated their own terms to the Bolsheviks. The Bolsheviks, in acute danger from Wrangel, could not refuse Polish demands; they may even have calculated, in the revolutionary mood of the period, that the more White Russian and Ukrainian territory was placed under the Poles, the greater the chance of a successful social and national revolt". ('The Russian-Polish Frontier', Special Article, *The Times*, 12 January 1944.)

29

In Appendix No. 5 we give an account from a Polish source of the failure to negotiate peace between Poland and Soviet Russia (May 1919–April 1920) and of the unfortunate Polish-Soviet war, as well as some idea of Polish policy and claims during and after the Paris Peace Conference.

Could the Polish-Soviet war have been avoided? "We can now see"—wrote Sir John Maynard in 1943—"that the answer is Yes, had the western powers not been themselves at war with the 'Reds', and had the threat of class-revolution not frightened and prejudiced people the world over. An offer of a friendly settlement was made by Moscow late in 1919 and repeated in the following January. Pilsudski began the war—was it done with support from the West?—certainly the Soviet leaders thought so, and from now on they regarded Poland as the willing instrument—let us say 'spearhead' of the capitalist powers."

The Polish-Soviet war was ended by an armistice and a preliminary treaty concluded on 12 October 1920. The Treaty of Riga was signed in the following March. It was recognized by the Allied Powers only two years later.

"Poland thus succeeded at Russia's expense in practically doubling the territory the Curzon Line would have given her." ". . . . A Polish occupation of these regions [White and Little Russian] means the hostility of every Russian, Bolshevik or Monarchist, Liberal or Reactionary." (Professor Temperley's *History of the Peace Conference of Paris*, published under the auspices of the British Institute of International Affairs, Oxford University Press, 1924, Vol. VI, pp. 322 & 278.)

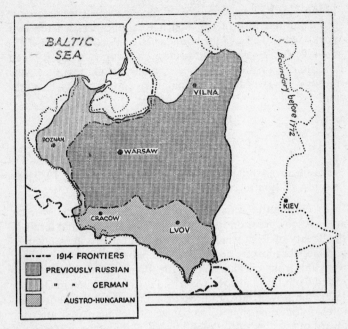

MAP V. Poland, 1921–1939

What was the percentage of Poles to the total population between the Curzon Line and the Riga frontier? On a liberal estimate (based on the Polish census of 1931), particulars of which the reader will find in Appendix No. 6, there were *hardly more than 20 to 23 per cent of Poles.**

---

* "At Riga Poland demanded and obtained as much White Russian and Ukrainian territory as she thought she would be able to assimilate integrally, and ever since has claimed this to be a supreme piece of moderation. Dmowski talked about a Great Power Poland as a 'barrier' between Germany and Russia, and an outpost of Western Europe against both. . . ." ('Russia and Poland', Special Article, *The Times*, 14 January 1944.) Even now, Roman Fengler, one of the leaders of the National Party (formerly Dmowski's Party), still speaks of the "far-reaching territorial concessions" made by Poland

Map No. V shows the three components that went to constitute the territory of the Polish Republic between the two World Wars. The eastern boundaries of Poland in 1667–1772 and 1921–1939, just as the western boundaries of the Russian Empire in 1914, were not ethnographic boundaries: they were traced by the sword and by diplomacy—not by self-determination.

30

Polish-Soviet relations from 1921 to September 1939 can be said to fall into certain periods:

(*a*) During the years up to 1927, relations between Warsaw and Moscow were on the whole correct: the essential terms of the Treaty of Riga were carried out, and many steps taken to regulate the normal contacts of neighbour nations, but they were far from cordial. When the Polish general Zeligowski seized from Lithuania the town and district of Vilna in October 1920, the Soviet Government disapproved of the action and refused for some time to recognize this change even after the award of the district to Poland by the Conference of Ambassadors in 1923.† The Polish attitude to the Soviet Note of protest

at Riga, and an official publication of the Polish Ministry of Information even goes so far as to say that "in the Riga Treaty of 1921 *Poland agreed to a frontier which left on the Soviet side five-sixths of the former Polish territory in the East*". (*Polish Fortnightly Review*, Editorial, No. 95, 1 July 1944—italics are ours.) But what is here meant by the former Polish territory, *five-sixths* of which were surrendered by Poland at Riga—the Jagellonian Empire at its maximum expansion in 1494 or the territories occupied by Poland for a score of years during the Conquest of Muscovy in the early seventeenth century?

† "The Polish claim rested, in point of nationality, upon the fact that the Polish element was larger than the Lithuanian element in Vilna City—where, however (as in many Polish towns), the Poles themselves were outnumbered by the Jews. Throughout the rest of the province the Polish population was numerically insignificant, though it included a larger proportion of the land-owning class. Juridically, the Polish claim rested on the decision of the Conference of Ambassadors, which was based on the provision in the Treaty of

of 5 April 1923 is well described in the words of Casimir Smogorzewski, the well-known Polish journalist, now editor of *Free Europe:* "Ne reconnaît pas qui veut. La Pologne ne répondit même pas à cette note, et l'affaire en resta là". (*La Pologne Restaurée*, Paris, 1927, p. 180.) Even more energetic was the protest of the Soviet Government, in its note of 10 May 1924, against violation of Article 7 of the Treaty of Riga (See Appendix No. 3, p. 60) safeguarding the linguistic and cultural autonomy of the Russians, White Russians and the Ukrainians in Polish territory.

The U.S.S.R. and Germany were both outside the League, and they had reached an understanding at Rapallo. German officers were helping to rebuild the Soviet armies. On the other hand, Poland was engaged in trying to form a Baltic to Black Sea Bloc, which was, as it still is, distasteful to the Soviet Government, if only for its popular name, the *cordon sanitaire*. It will be remembered that these were the years of active efforts of the Comintern abroad.

(*b*) Relations began to improve in the period 1928-1932. These years saw the adherence of both powers to the Briand-Kellogg Pact to outlaw war, and the example set by the U.S.S.R. and Poland in implementing that plan in a local area, by the Litvinov Protocol. The middle of 1932 brought the Polish-Soviet Pact of Non-aggression, following on which, twelve months later, came the 'Convention for the Definition of an Aggressor'. To it eight states subscribed, including Rumania. All this amounted to a distinct improvement in the atmosphere in Eastern Europe, at the same time marking the

Versailles (Art. 87) to the effect that 'the boundaries of Poland not laid down in the present Treaty will be subsequently determined by the Principal Allied and Associated Powers'. In the case of Vilna, as in that of Bessarabia, it is difficult to avoid the conclusion that the Allied Powers had placed themselves in a difficult legal position by making over to a third party former Russian territory of which they had no apparent right to dispose." (*Survey of International Affairs*, 1920–1923, by Arnold J. Toynbee. Published under the auspices of the British Institute of International Affairs. Oxford University Press. 1927. Page 256. See also pages 250 to 256.)

entry of the new regime in Russia into the field of international affairs after ten years of virtual isolation.

(c) Then came the shadow of Hitler Germany. In January 1934 Poland secured a Non-aggression Pact with Berlin. "The Polish *refroidissement* towards France and *rapprochement* towards Germany . . . was one of the most remarkable of the political phenomena in Europe during the years 1933 and 1934. . . ." (Professor Toynbee.)

In November of the same year Poland repudiated by a unilateral declaration the Minorities Treaty of 28 June 1919, signed by her at Versailles and guaranteed by the League of Nations, although seven of its clauses 'contained fundamental laws, never to be altered by Poland'. [See Appendix No. 3, pp. 59–60.]

The way was now open, Germany having left the League, for the Soviet Union to join it, and to become Europe's most ardent advocate of the principle of collective security. Its proposal of an Eastern Locarno, which was not liked by the Germans, was on that account rejected by Poland. The position of Poland now looked equivocal.

(d) In March 1938 came a clash between Poland and the Soviet Union over the ultimatum presented by Poland to Lithuania.*

Six months later, in September, when Czechoslovakia was attacked by Germany, the Poles seized Teschen, after an attempt made by the Soviet Government to prevent the seizure.

---

* This ultimatum was delivered six days after Germany's seizure of Austria. Polish divisions were moved towards Lithuanian frontiers. The Soviet Government informed the Polish Ambassador in Moscow that "in the event of armed action against Lithuania it would reserve the right to act". (*War and the Working Class*, Moscow, 15 January 1944, p. 10.)

"Although the ultimatum to Lithuania", writes Stanislaw Mackiewicz, "was sent without any German co-operation, it certainly had its source in the Anschluss and the general parallelism which existed at the time between German and Polish policy". (*Colonel Beck and his policy*, Eyre & Spottiswoode, London, 1944, p. 118.)

40

The Soviet Government notified the Poles that they no longer regarded their treaties with them as binding.* Thereafter, late in November, they reversed that declaration by issuing the joint Soviet-Polish statement re-asserting the continuance of the non-aggression treaty between them.

The last months of the year also saw the attempt of the Polish Foreign Minister to encourage a further partitioning of Czechoslovakia, when he 'tried to persuade King Carol to incorporate in Rumania the eastern extremity of Carpathian Ruthenia, simultaneously with the occupation by Hungary of the rest of this province' (S. Mackiewicz).

(e) The year 1939 witnessed the occupation of Prague by the Germans; the failure of British and French negotiations with Moscow—due in part to the unwillingness of the Poles to accept terms involving the appearance of Soviet armies on their territory, in part to the claims of the U.S.S.R. in regard to the Baltic States—and the conclusion on 23 August of the German-Soviet Treaty. At the end of September half of Poland was in German hands, the other half occupied by the Red Army. It is not difficult to find reasons for the decision of the Soviet High Command to advance their armies into Poland on the

---

* "On 21 September the Polish Minister in Prague presented a Note demanding that the question of territories inhabited by the Polish minority should be settled in the same manner as that of the territories inhabited by Germans, and denouncing the Treaty of 23 April 1925. . . . Immediately after the Munich Agreement, on 30 September, Poland sent Czechoslovakia a Note, in the form of an ultimatum with a twenty-four-hour time-limit, demanding the cession of part of the Teschen district". The Czechoslovak Government acceded to this demand—'in consideration of the grave international situation and under stress of circumstances arising out of the Munich decision'. The Polish occupation was carried out immediately. The district occupied by Poland contained a larger number of Czechs than of Poles. (*Documents on International Affairs*, 1938. Edited by Monica Curtis and issued under the auspices of the Royal Institute of International Affairs. 1943. Vol. II, p. 324.)

On 23 September, the Soviet Government gave an official warning to the Polish Chargé d'Affaires in Moscow that, in the event of Polish troops entering the territory of Czechoslovakia, the Governments of the U.S.S.R. would regard this as an act of unwarranted aggression and would immediately denounce the Soviet–Polish Pact of Non-aggression of 1932. (Cf. *War and the Working Class*, Moscow, 1 October 1943, p. 14.)

morning of 17 September, ostensibly for the protection of the Ukrainian and White Russian peoples. Those of strategy alone would suffice. (See Section 32: Mr. Churchill's statement of 1 October 1939.)

* * *

The following justifications of the Vilna and Teschen affairs, and of the Soviet occupation of Eastern Poland have been advanced:

Occupation of Vilna, 1920. "General Zeligowski's sudden act of insubordination is explicable by reasons of immediate utility to the Polish cause. It was not a ruse of war and not a clumsy pretext for an unwarranted act of violence. Underlying was a much deeper political scheme. The general belief at the time, confirmed by later evidence, was that the person really responsible for Zeligowski's conduct was no other than the Chief of the Polish State himself [Pilsudski]. It was his cherished desire to restore something of the ancient unity of Poland and Lithuania. That was why he wished to set up Vilna and its region as an independent factor capable of playing the part of intermediary and eventually becoming a link between the two countries". (The Polish Research Centre, *The Story of Wilno*, London, 1942, pp. 24–25.)

Occupation of Teschen, 1938. "An ultimatum [sent by Poland] at the end of September brought an answer from Dr. Benesh in the affirmative and the territory in question was taken over by the Poles just in time to keep the Nazi troops out. All this looked both unkind and unjust, but the appearance and the reality are different. The Poles saw further than those who condemned their action, and saved 120,000 of their own people as well as fifty miles of one of the trunk railway lines of Central Europe from getting into Nazi hands". (*Poland*, by Professor W. J. Rose, Penguin Books, 1939, p. 232.)

Occupation of Eastern Poland, 1939. ". . . The Russians without scruple took the chance offered to them, justifying themselves by the plea that the Polish Government were now seeking cover in Rumania and that therefore they had to look after their own interests and those of the White Russian and Ukrainian populations in Poland. Even the British Government, when in 1920 it had proposed the 'Curzon Line' had recognized that this territory was not properly Polish, and if Germany had completed her conquest of Poland, she would have been annexing a population that belonged to Russia". (*Russia*, by Professor Bernard Pares, Penguin Books, 1940, p. 242.)*

31

Thus, in September 1939, the U.S.S.R. gained all the territories east of the Curzon Line and in addition Przemysl and the district of Bialystok. The city and region of Vilna were ceded by Russia to Lithuania. Eastern Galicia, unlike the rest of the territory acquired, had not been within the confines of the Modern Russian State.

Having held hurriedly organised elections in the occupied territories, the Soviet Government incorporated these territories in the U.S.S.R. The thirteen million inhabitants were declared to be Soviet citizens. The Soviet economic system was introduced in regard both to agriculture and urban property, in some places with more, in others with less vigour. The number of deportations is a matter of controversy, but it was large.

The Polish Government, reconstructed in France, issued a protest against plebiscites carried out by an occupying Power and held according to the Communist version of self-determination, declaring them contrary to international law. (It will be remembered that in 1920 no attempt whatsoever was made by the Polish Government to hold plebiscites in these regions.)

* The military considerations underlying the Soviet occupation of Poland are discussed in *The Russian Campaigns of 1941–43*, by W. E. D. Allen and Paul Muratoff, Penguin Books, 1944, pp. 23 and 25.

In his broadcast of 1 October 1939, Mr. Churchill said: "We could have wished that the Russian armies should be standing on the present line as the friends and allies of Poland, instead of as invaders. But that the Russian armies should stand on this line was clearly necessary for the safety of Russia against the Nazi menace".

On 19 October 1939, the Under-Secretary of State for Foreign Affairs, Mr. Butler, referring to the Anglo-Polish Agreement of 25 August 1939, made the following statement: "During the negotiations which led up to the signature of the Agreement, it was understood between the Polish Government and His Majesty's Government that the Agreement should only cover the case of aggression by Germany; and the Polish Government confirm that this is so". (*Hansard*, House of Commons, 19.10.1939: Col. 1082.)

The Secretary of State for Foreign Affairs, Lord Halifax, in his speech in the House of Lords on 26 October 1939, said: "The last thing I would wish to do in this matter is to defend the action of the Soviet Government at the particular time at which they took it. But it is right to remember two things: Firstly, that they would never have taken that action if the German Government had not started it and set the example that they did set when they invaded Poland without any declaration of war. In the second place, it is perhaps, as a matter of historical interest, worth recalling that the action of the Soviet Government has been to advance the Russian boundary to what was substantially the boundary recommended at the time of the Versailles Conference by the noble Marquess who used to lead the House, Lord Curzon, who was then Foreign Secretary." (*Hansard*, House of Lords, 26.10.1939: Col. 1565.)

Referring to Polish-Soviet relations in his statement in the House of Commons on 22 February 1944, Mr. Churchill said: ". . . I may remind the House that we ourselves have never in the past guaranteed, on behalf of His Majesty's Government, any particular frontier line to Poland. We did not approve of the Polish occupation of Vilna in 1920. The British view in 1919 stands expressed in the so-called Curzon Line which attempted to deal, at any rate partially, with the problem". (*Hansard*, House of Commons, 22.2.1944: Col. 698.)

33

We come now to the last act of the drama. On 22 June 1941 the German armies launched a grand attack on the Soviet Union. The latter was at once welcomed by Mr. Churchill as an Ally in full standing, and on the following day the Head of the Polish Government in exile, General Sikorski, expressed in a broadcast the hope that the U.S.S.R. would return to its position dating from September 1918 of goodwill towards a free and independent Poland. A month later, after much negotiation, the Polish-Soviet Agreement was signed in London, the first clause of which reads: "The Government of the U.S.S.R. recognizes the Soviet-German treaties of 1939 as to territorial changes in Poland as having lost their validity. The Polish Government declares that Poland is not bound by any agreement with any third Power, which is directed against the U.S.S.R." The second clause provided for the immediate restoration of diplomatic relations, and the fourth for the creation of a Polish Army on Soviet soil, to share in the war against the common enemy. On the same day, the British Foreign Minister handed General Sikorski a note, the concluding sentence of which read: "I also desire to assure you that His Majesty's Government do not recognize any territorial changes which have been effected in Poland since August 1939".

34

The Agreement at once brought some amelioration in Polish-Soviet relations. The following testimony of Professor Stanislaw Grabski can illustrate this: ". . . I must do the authorities of the Soviet Commissariat for Internal Affairs justice. At the time [early autumn of 1941], notwithstanding the great difficulties of communication caused by the war, they did endeavour as quickly as possible to restore the rights of free Polish citizens to the majority of those inhabitants of the eastern half of Poland arrested and deported between September 1939 and June 1941—irrespective of their nationality or religion". (S. Grabski, *The Polish-Soviet Frontier*, London, 1943, p. 5.)*

This improvement of Polish-Russian relations was, however, short-lived. For a number of causes, which we cannot discuss here, there was in 1942 an increasing deterioration in those relations, which, early in 1943, found expression in an article by the Ukrainian Soviet leader (later Assistant People's Commissar for Foreign Affairs) A. E. Korneichuk, who severely criticized the Poles and Polish propaganda abroad.†

In April 1943 the Katyn incident brought about a break of diplomatic relations between the Soviet Government and the Polish Government in London. (See pp. 75–83.)

In January 1944 the Soviet Government repeated its pledge for the 're-establishment of a strong and independent Poland' and expressed its willingness to conclude an alliance, if the Polish people wished it, between the U.S.S.R. and Poland against Germany. As a basis for the future frontier between the two countries, it offered the Curzon Line, suggesting at the same time that 'Poland's western borders should be extended through the incorporation in Poland of ancient Polish land previously wrested by Germany.' (See pp. 85–87.)

The reply of the Polish Government to this offer did not prove satisfactory to the Soviet Government, who declared on 17 January 1944 that in the Polish reply 'the question of the recognition of the Curzon Line as the Soviet-Polish

* Cf. also A. Y. Vyshinski's statement on (i) The Polish Army Units in the U.S.S.R.; (ii) Measures for relief to Polish families (see full text in *Soviet War News*, No. 556, 8 May 1943).

† See full text in *Soviet War News*, No. 496, 28 February 1943.

frontier is entirely evaded and ignored, which can only be interpreted as a rejection of the Curzon Line'. (See pp. 87–88).

On 24 May 1944, Mr. Churchill in his speech in the House of Commons declared: "I must repeat that the essential part of any arrangement [between Russia and Poland] is regulation of the Polish eastern frontier, and that, in return for any withdrawal made by Poland in that quarter, she should receive other territories at the expense of Germany, which will give her an ample seaboard and a good, adequate and reasonable homeland in which the Polish nation may safely dwell." (*Hansard*, House of Commons, 24.5.1944: Col. 778.)

On 28 September 1944, Mr. Churchill said: "Territorial changes on the frontiers of Poland there will have to be. Russia has a right to our support in this matter, because it is the Russian armies which alone can deliver Poland from the German talons; and after all the Russian people have suffered at the hands of Germany they are entitled to safe frontiers and to have a friendly neighbour on their western flank." (*Hansard*, House of Commons, 28.9.1944: Cols. 489–90.)

The relevant documents referring to events in April 1943 and January 1944 will be found in Appendix No. 7.

35

In this broad historical survey of Russo-Polish relations from the early times to the spring of 1944, our chief aim has been to bring out and elucidate the century-old fundamental issue at stake between the two countries—the crucial problem of the 'Western Lands'. A just and final solution of this problem should solve all the others, which—at least in the view of the editor—are all of them of a more or less secondary and transient nature. They demand a separate study carried out on a different scale and are naturally beyond the scope of this brief outline.

We will conclude with the summing up of the Russo-Polish problem as presented in *The Times* ('Russia and Poland', Special Article, 14 January 1944):

"Poland carries a grievous burden in her geographical contours and historical heritage. In the west, her vital and indefeasible ethnic claims lacerate the body of Prussia: in the east, memories and traditions, and doubtful and dwindling assets inherited from the old republic embroil her with the White Russians and the Ukrainians, and through them with Russia. Polish sway over those vast eastern territories resembled the 'Protestant ascendancy' in southern Ireland, and was equally untenable; but a century of political submersion rendered it infinitely more difficult for the Poles to comprehend the change which the rise of the masses to political life was producing in the national character of those territories. Moreover, the Polish 'gentry' in those eastern borderlands were a far more numerous class than, for instance, the German barons in the Baltic provinces or the Anglo-Irish landed gentry; they were neither conquerors nor intruders but mostly as autochthonous as the peasantries, from whom they had become estranged in language and religion by a gradual process of cultural absorption into the gentry class. . . .

"The folly of the Franco-Polish system of 1920, which tried both to encircle Germany and to draw a *cordon sanitaire* round Russia, recreated an understanding between the two. This was broken by Hitler's advent. Russia entered the League of Nations and was ready to co-operate with Western Europe and Poland against Nazi Germany; for a while France, under Barthou, the last of the Triple Entente statesmen, was willing to join hands with Russia. But not so Pilsudski or his epigones. Russia was cold-shouldered, especially during the Munich period, and even for some time after Prague; once more a Russian-German agreement was concluded. And for a third time Germany destroyed her own chances—by prematurely attacking Russia. . . .

"The friendship of Russia enabled Bismarck to erect the mighty edifice of the Second Reich: the estrangement between the Western Powers and Russia enabled Hitler and his Third Reich to attain predominance in Europe. But German predominance is at least as dangerous to Russia as to the West: for, while the Germans try to vanquish the West, they are out to conquer and acquire the East of Europe, the traditional 'space' for their 'colonization'.

"It is in the vital interest of both Poland and Russia, and, indeed, of all Europe, that the old Russian-Polish feud now be settled for good and all. Such a settlement between Russia and Poland would best be secured by a frontier which either way left no substantial bodies of men on the wrong side: this might involve some voluntary transfer of populations. A clean frontier and non-interference in each other's internal affairs, social or national, must be the basis for future friendship and co-operation".

36

When these pages were already in proof, Mr. Churchill, on his return from Moscow, gave utterance to 'words of hope, reinforced by confidence', with which we are happy to conclude our survey. "Although I do not underrate the difficulties which remain", said the Prime Minister in his speech in the House of Commons on 27 October, "it is a comfort to feel that Britain and Soviet Russia, and I do not doubt the United States, are all firmly agreed in the recreation of a strong, free, independent, sovereign Poland loyal to the allies and friendly to her great neighbour and liberator, Russia. Speaking more particularly for his Majesty's Government, it is our persevering and constant aim that the Polish people, after their suffering and vicissitudes, shall find in Europe an abiding home and resting place, which, though it may not entirely coincide or correspond with the pre-war frontier of Poland, will, nevertheless, be adequate for the needs of the Polish nation and not inferior in character and quality, taking the picture as a whole, to what they had previously possessed."

APPENDIX I

(*Reference: Sections* 8, 9 *and* 10)

POLISH INTERVENTION IN RUSSIA (*XVIIth CENTURY*)

The Polish and the Russian interpretations of the events and policies at the end of the sixteenth and the beginning of the seventeenth centuries are given below (*a* and *b* are Polish; *c* is Russian), as well as a quotation from an essay by Lord Robert Cecil, later Marquess of Salisbury (*d*).

(*a*) "Polish ideas began to influence life in the Russian State from the fifteenth century. At the beginning of the seventeenth century, Polish influence was so strong that the Russian boyars offered the crown to the son of the King of Poland. Polish policy was, however, hesitant and vacillating. 'In fact', writes Z. L. Zaleski in his book *Dilemme Russo-Polonais*, 'there were then in Poland two very distinct Muscovite policies. One faithful to the Polish-Lithuanian tradition, wise and conciliatory, without aiming at conquest, desired to settle all differences amicably and to form a great alliance of Poland and Moscow against Islam. Such was the policy of the Chancellor Jan Zamoyski, of King Stephen Bathory (1576–1586), and especially of the Hetman Zolkiewski. The other, the policy of King Sigismund III Wasa (1587–1632), born of the successes of the Polish armies, based on ambition and pride, was *Catholic* rather than *national*, and its result was to aggravate the constant differences between the two countries'. In the seventeenth century, the Empire of the Tsars initiated a policy of 'uniting all Russian territories' and of interfering in Polish affairs."

(Casimir Smogorzewski, *La Pologne Restaurée*. Gebethner & Wolff, Paris, 1927, pp. 138–139.)

(*b*) ". . . Bathory died after three successful campaigns against the Muscovites and it was this Eastern danger which especially pre-occupied Bathory's successors. In 1610, during the reign of Sigismund III Wasa, the Polish army had entered Moscow, and the boyars had proclaimed Vladislav IV, Sigismund's son, as the Tsar. But the King, owing to religious scruples, failed to take action and thus lost the opportunity of uniting Muscovy to Poland. This bril-

liant campaign resulted merely in some territorial concessions."
(*Petite Encyclopédie Polonaise.* General Editor: Erasme Piltz;
editors: E. Woroniecki, S. S. Zaleski, J. Perlowski. Payot & Co.,
Lausanne-Paris, 1916, p. 21.)

(*c*) i. ". . . The Union of Lublin in 1569, joining Lithuanian
Russia with Poland, turned the Lithuanian question into a Polish
one and gave rise to open competition and strife between the two
Slav (Polish and Russian) peoples. At first luck was on the side of
the Poles. . . . Success inspired King Stephen Bathory. Together
with the Jesuit Possevin he had already worked out a grandiose
plan for conquering the whole of Muscovy. While Stephen Bathory
dreamed of turning the State of Muscovy into a Polish province by
means of the sword, Possevin, with the cross in his hand, dreamed of
making the Russian land an obedient and faithful daughter of the
Church of Rome. . . .

ii. ". . . The Time of Troubles opened up new possibilities for the
Poles . . . the plans of Bathory seemed to be nearing fulfilment; but
the inspired patriotism of Minin and Pozharsky saved Russia from
the danger of losing her political independence.

iii. "The difficult task of liquidating the grievous heritage of the
Time of Troubles fell to the lot of the new Romanov dynasty. The
process of liquidation, although it cost Russia two wars, did not
give satisfactory results. The first war (1613-1618) ended at Deulino
with an armistice of $14\frac{1}{2}$ years. It did not settle the dispute: the
Smolensk and Seversk regions remained in Polish hands, Prince
Vladislav continued to call himself the Tsar of Muscovy; the Poles,
as previously, would not recognize the new order established in the
country. . . . The Peace of Polyanovka (1634) restored normal relations with Poland: the process of liquidation had been accomplished,
but at the price of completely renouncing the Smolensk and Seversk
regions."

(Professor E. Shmurlo. *Historia Rossii.* 1922, pp. 217–219.)

(*d*) The partition of Russian territory by Sweden and Poland at
the beginning of the seventeenth century ". . . took place in the
century previous to the partition of Poland, and was parallel to it
from many points of view. Both were carefully timed so as to take
advantage of a period of internal anarchy. Both began by seating
the nominee of the partitioning power upon the throne of the

country, and ended by a seizure of territory. Both were undertaken with the professed object of advancing the interests of a religious creed as well as those of an ambitious dynasty. Both were open to the reproach of disregarding treaty engagements. They only differed in one point. Catherine united to her empire populations who already belonged to its race and religion; Sigismund annexed to his kingdom populations who were alien to it in both. Yet the heinousness of Catherine's proceedings has almost passed into a political axiom, while the world has heard very little of Sigismund's misdeeds.

There has been no emigration of Russian nobles to tell the tale of it in fancy colours in every European capital; no powerful Church to lament, under the guise of a sympathy for the oppressed, the miscarried hopes of a military propaganda."

('Poland' [by the Marquess of Salisbury], *Quarterly Review*, 1863, Vol. 113, p. 458.)

APPENDIX 2
(*Reference: Section* 13)

RUSSIAN INTERVENTION IN POLAND (XVIIIth CENTURY)

The general view on the partition of Poland by Prussia, Austria and Russia is well known. It is condemned by most historians as an eighteenth century crime, which even the rebirth of Poland in 1918 only reduced—in the opinion of W. F. Reddaway—"from murder to a murderous assault . . . no 'happy ending', however, can justify the would-be assassins of historic Poland in what an indulgent judge could palliate only by styling it a case of lynching. . . . ." (*The Cambridge History of Poland.* 1941. p. 88.)

From the point of view of Russia's national interest the question of Poland's partition was discussed by the famous Russian historian, Professor V. O. Klyuchevsky, who at the end of the last century in his lectures at the University of Moscow, stressed the fact that the political destruction of Poland was not in the interest of Russia. For Russia it was a question—the old question—of recovering her Western Lands. But the failure to keep this object clearly in view led to the distortion of the whole problem and resulted in the destruction of Poland and the establishment of a Prussian frontier on the Niemen, without the restoration to Russia of the whole of the Western Lands (since Galicia passed to another Power). "The direct interest of Russia required not the destruction of Poland, but the reunion of the Western Lands. History made it incumbent on Russia to get back from Poland all Russian territory in the latter's possession, not to share Poland with two German states. . . . Poland should have been made into a real Polish Poland instead of into a German one."

At the present time the Russian point of view can be summed up as follows: "Although we by no means wish to justify the eighteenth century Partition of Poland, which deprived Poland of political independence, we do not consider it to have been unjust in so far as it freed the Ukrainians and White Russians from the Polish domination and enabled them to achieve re-union with their brothers on the other side of the frontier". (*War and the Working Class*, No. 7, p. 12, 1 April 1944, Moscow—article by N. Malinin.)

In this connection it is of interest to recall a little-known essay of Lord Robert Cecil (later Marquess of Salisbury, Prime Minister), in which he attempts to separate the Polish-Russian problem from the question of the dismemberment of Poland as such.

". . . The ordinary mode of dealing with the question [of Partitions] is to ignore all history before the eighteenth century. At that epoch two countries forced themselves upon the attention of Western Europe. One was weak and decaying, torn by factions, and a prey to foreign intrigue. The other was strong and growing, and, under the guidance of a prince of marvellous ability, was gaining a dangerous ascendancy over its weaker neighbour. As the century went on, the strong Power suddenly proceeded to tear away a large slice from the territory of the weak Power; and other neighbours doing the same thing at the same time, the weak Power ceased to exist. Viewed in this way by itself, without any reference to the history that had gone before, the partition appears in colours almost as dark as those in which the Polish emigrants have painted it. It is not surprising that contemporary Europe, to whom the Polish question was a new acquaintance, should have quietly contented themselves with this view of the case. If they had been watching the relations of the Poles and Russians for centuries, as they had watched those of the French and Germans, they would probably have taken a different view of the moral aspect of the affair. They would have seen that the conquest was but a re-conquest; that the transactions that were passing before their eyes were but the closing scene of a long and varied drama; and that the mass of the inhabitants of the annexed provinces, far from being robbed of their freedom and their country, were only being reunited to those of their own race and their own religion from whom the ambition of the Polish nobles had severed them for so long . . . "

". . . When, after half a century of trouble, the Russians recovered the territory and the political peace they had enjoyed before Sigismund sent the first false Demetrius among them, it was not unnatural that Russian diplomacy should take an active interest in the vacancies of the Polish throne."

". . . It was not Russia who first commenced the system of meddling in the elections of Polish Kings; nor did she adopt it until, by leaving the use of the Polish army to be scrambled for by others, she had laid herself open to an insidious and well-nigh deadly blow. Nor did she begin the perilous game of fighting a rival race by tampering with the succession to its throne. A contest fought upon such a plan could only end in the disorganisation and political death of one of the contending parties. Poland chose the weapons for that deadly duel. It does not lie in her mouth to protest against them now, simply because she could not use them so skilfully as her antagonist."

". . . Undoubtedly a sovereign of a quixotic temperament, with an imagination sufficiently strong to discover matter for admiration in the Government of the Polish nobility, might have made war with Prussia and Austria to preserve the integrity of Poland. Those who have watched the course of a more modern experiment to keep 'sick men' alive by the force of a foreign guarantee, will form their own judgment as to the probable success or advantage of such a policy. Catherine was, undoubtedly, very far removed from being a quixotic sovereign. But the course she took was, at all events, one of which the Poles, who for centuries had been a conquering race and who had generally conquered at the expense of Russia, had no right whatever to complain. She effaced the last vestige of Polish domination in Russia. She re-united to the rest of the Russian race the Russians who for centuries had been under the yoke of Poland. She occupied what still remained under Polish sway of the country of the Niemen and Dnieper, which centuries before had belonged to the empire of Wladimir and Jaroslaw. But she did not seize a single acre of genuinely Polish ground. . . ."

". . . The line which divided the two kingdoms of Boleslas and Wladimir may be roughly described as starting about fifty miles to the east of Memel, and going straight down due south till it struck the Carpathian mountain-range. It coincides very nearly with the frontier which, some eight centuries later, Catherine obtained for the Russian Empire just before her death. The only difference between the two frontiers is, that the ancient one was about fifty miles more favourable to Russia than the modern. . . ."

'Poland' [by the Marquess of Salisbury], *The Quarterly Review*. Vol. 113, 1863, pp. 452, 453, 459, 464).

With reference to the preceding paragraphs, we add the following quotation:

". . . Both the White Russians and the Ukrainians—also called Little Russians or Ruthenians—are unquestionably far nearer ethnographically to the Great Russians than to the Poles. . . . These territories [White Russia and Eastern Galicia] were unquestionably originally a substantial part of the first Russian state of Kiev. . . . When in the seventeenth and eighteenth centuries Russia recovered the White Russian area, she certainly regarded herself as recovering what was her own: indeed in the partitions of Poland, Catherine II did not appropriate any dominantly Polish territory. . . ."

(Professor Bernard Pares and Professor Seton-Watson, Editorial note in the *Slavonic Review*, Vol. VIII, June 1929, pp. 51–52.)

APPENDIX 3

(*Reference: Section* 27)

EASTERN GALICIA AND THE PEACE CONFERENCE

We give here a few extracts on the question of Eastern Galicia from Professor H. W. V. Temperley's *History of the Peace Conference of Paris*, published under the auspices of the British Institute of International Affairs in 1924. (Oxford University Press.) The quotations below are from Vol. VI, ch. 2—*Poland at the Peace Conference* by Professor H. J. Paton. For more comprehensive information on the subject—in particular on the Ukrainian problem, which is not discussed by us—the reader should consult this article (pp. 233–283), and Professor Sumner's *Survey of Russian History* (pp. 222–235.)

"As regards the international status of this country, Austria ceded the whole of Galicia to the Principal Allied and Associated Powers by the Treaty of St. Germain in September 1919. The Principal Allied and Associated Powers assigned Western Galicia to Poland by the 'Certain Frontiers' Treaty which they signed at Sèvres on 10 August 1920, but the Poles refused to sign this Treaty apparently on the ground that they could not accept any separate treatment for Eastern Galicia. The whole of Galicia and certainly Eastern Galicia, is still in international law the property of the Principal Allied and Associated Powers. [Written before the assignment of E. Galicia to Poland in March 1923.]

"It may be said at once that there was never any intention on the part of any of the Great Powers to exclude the whole of Eastern Galicia from Poland. The solid Polish bloc crosses the division between Western and Eastern Galicia and extends to the line of the River San. The line which the British Delegation proposed as the Eastern frontier of Poland proper in this area, ran to the east of that river and included in Poland the whole solidly Polish area besides a strip of mountainous country in the south inhabited by the Lemkians, a body of mountaineers whose national affinities and sympathies were all with Russia but whose geographical situation rendered it apparently inevitable that they should remain within the Polish frontiers." (pp. 266–267.)

57

"In the sense here adopted Eastern Galicia is an area of slightly under 50,000 sq. kilometres. Its inhabitants number slightly over four and a half millions—a number sufficiently large to render its ultimate fate of very serious importance. Of these—to judge by the [Austrian] census of religions—just under 3,000,000 or 63 per cent are Ruthenians, just over 1,000,000 or 23 per cent are Poles, and a little over 500,000 or 12 per cent are Jews. The linguistic census includes most of the Jews among the Poles. . . . The Ruthenians maintain that the number of Poles is greatly exaggerated and that Poles are in reality only some 500,000 or 600,000. It is, however, safer to accept the census in spite of its Polish bias and to regard the Poles as constituting something under a quarter of the whole population, nearly two-thirds of which is composed of Ruthenians." (pp. 267–268.)

[According to estimates by C. Smogorzewski (*Free Europe*, 7 and 21 April 1944), based on the 1931 *Polish census*, the population of Eastern Galicia amounted to four and three quarter millions and was divided as follows:

According to religious denominations:

Uniates (Greek Catholics)	just over	2,850,000 or 60 per cent
Roman Catholics	„	1,350,000 or 28·5 per cent
Jews	„	490,000 or 10 per cent

According to languages:

Ukrainians	just over	2,500,000 or 53 per cent
Poles	„	1,850,000 or 39 per cent
Jews	just under	350,000 or 7 per cent

Round figures are given here.—EDITOR'S NOTE.]

"The distribution of the two chief races is very mixed. There is a considerable Polish minority almost everywhere and in places even in the country districts the Poles are actually in majority . . . Lemberg [Lvov] itself and the country round it are in majority Polish, and there are certain areas, curiously enough in the extreme east, where the Poles are in a definite majority. Eastern Galicia is in short a Ruthenian sea with a large number of Polish islands rising above the surface in a curiously irregular manner." (p. 268.)

". . . In May 1919 the Poles attacked successfully and the Polish advance stopped after protests from Paris only when the greater part of Eastern Galicia had been occupied by Polish troops. Subsequently (on 19 June) the Poles were authorized to continue their advance to the borders of Eastern Galicia on the ground, which later events hardly confirmed, that what remained of the Galician-Ukrainian army was no longer in a position to resist the Bolshevik army which at that time appeared to be engaged in an attempt to join up with the Hungarians. The British proposal that at the same time a High Commissioner should be appointed by the Allies to safeguard the interests of the Ruthenians was rejected. The Poles thus received authorization from Paris for a military occupation of Eastern Galicia modified only by some vague references to ultimate self-determination; and although this was not intended to prejudice the final political decision, it committed the Conference to a Polish solution of the question, until such time as the final decision should be taken." (pp. 272–3.)

". . . It is useless to disguise the fact that the Poles, by presenting the Conference with a *fait accompli* in Eastern Galicia, materially affected the settlement." (p. 245; see also Vol. I, pp. 335–8 and Vol. IV, pp. 84–5, 95, 103–5, 135.)*

On 15 March 1923 the Principal Allied Powers (Great Britain, France, Italy and Japan), under Article 87 of the Treaty of Versailles, assigned Eastern Galicia to Poland.

In reply to the question put in the House of Commons by Sir John Simon concerning the conditions subject to which this decision had been arrived at, the Prime Minister (Mr. Bonar Law) said: "The conditions are that Poland, which has been in occupation of the country for three or four years, has recognized that the ethnographical conditions make autonomy necessary in that region." (*Hansard*, House of Commons, 20.3.1923: Col. 2317.)

However, "no attempt has ever been made by Poland to fulfil the pledge of local autonomy which conditioned the cession to her of Eastern Galicia". (David Lloyd George, *The Truth about the Peace Treaties*, Gollancz, 1938, Vol. II, p. 1396; see also pp. 312–3, 992–4, 1394–6.)

In 1934 the Polish Government repudiated by a unilateral declaration the Minorities Treaty signed at Versailles in 1919. This Treaty

* In the view of Casimir Smogorzewski (*Free Europe*, 7 April 1944, p. 106), already by the end of 1919 "the question of Eastern Galicia had to all intents and purposes been settled in the international plane. By withdrawing (22 December 1919) its draft for the autonomous statute of Eastern Galicia . . . the Supreme Council *de facto* recognised Polish sovereignty in that province".

contained 12 clauses, of which 7 were recognized by Poland 'as fundamental laws', clause 1 providing that "no law, regulation or official action shall conflict or interfere with these stipulations, nor shall any law, regulation or official action prevail over them".*

In 1935 a new electoral law was introduced in Poland, which "made it virtually impossible for anyone to enter Parliament without the consent of the Government". (*Polish Fortnightly Review*, published by the Polish Ministry of Information in London, No. 81, 1 December 1943, p. 5—article by W. Kulerski, spokesman of the Polish Peasant Party.)

The difficulties involved in the solution of the Ukrainian problem were summed up in 1939 by Professor W. J. Rose as follows: "(1) The practical difficulty caused by the presence of a large Polish Minority in the Ukrainian areas: reaching as high as 40 per cent around Tarnopol; (2) The fear, rising from distrust, existing in the minds of millions of Poles, that the demand for autonomy is but a step in the direction of complete independence . . . ;(3) The pride,

---

* E.g. one of these special clauses (No. 7) stipulated that:

". . . Differences of religion, creed or confession shall not prejudice any Polish national in matters relating to the enjoyment of civil or political rights, as, for instance, admission to public employments, functions and honours, or the exercise of professions and industries. No restriction shall be imposed on the free use by any Polish national of any language in private intercourse, in commerce, in religion, in the Press or in publications of any kind, or at any meetings. . . . Adequate facilities shall be given to Polish nationals of non-Polish speech for the use of their language, either orally or in writing, before the Courts."

The rights of minorities (in fact *majorities* in most of the districts east of the Curzon Line) were safeguarded also in the Treaty of Riga (1921). Clause 7 provided among other things that persons of Ukrainian, White Russian and Russian nationality in Poland are entitled, "within the limits of the State laws, to employ their native tongue, organize and maintain their own schools, foster their own culture and form societies and unions for this purpose."

How conditions actually developed in some parts of the Western Lands may be inferred from the appearance of the following lines in the *Gazeta Poleska* (3 April 1938): "The only language permitted in Polesie in government institutions, municipalities, churches, schools, courts of law is the Polish language. . . . The use of the Russian language by Russians in Polesie is *to be considered a crime*". (From Prof. D. Odinets' article in *Sovremennye Zapiski*, No. LXX, Paris, p. 256.) The statement is particularly striking in view of the fact that in the Voyevodship of Polesie (an area roughly equal to Holland) the bulk of the population was non-Polish: according to the Polish census of 1931, out of 1,132,000 inhabitants only 11–14 per cent were Poles (125,000 on the basis of religion; 164,000 on the basis of language).

with which many Poles declare that Poland is a nation state; and would not readily accept any action that has the effect of conceding equality of dignity and status to any other people inside its borders. They would be shocked if anyone could be able to say that the new commonwealth is a 'nationality' state. One may be either amused or annoyed by this point of view, but it is there and cannot be ignored." (*Poland*, Penguin Books, 1939, p. 177.)

Writing in 1944, Professor O. Halecki (History expert in the Polish delegation to the Paris Peace Conference) states that now "the Poles themselves have become fully aware that the inconsistent pre-war policy towards the Ukrainians must be replaced by a constructive programme of co-operation, including autonomy for the regions where our Slavic minorities live in compact groups, and full opportunities for their cultural and economic development everywhere". ('The Post-war Poland', *The Slavonic Review*, American Series, Vol. 3, May 1944, p. 32.)

APPENDIX 4

(*Reference: Section* 28)

LORD CURZON'S NOTE OF 11 JULY 1920

In view of contemporary controversies about the precise signifi-
cance and scope of the Curzon Line, it may be useful to quote from
Lord Curzon's note to Mr. Chicherin, which was sent from Spa on
11 July 1920, with the approval of the Allied Powers (and Poland).*
The Note proposed:

"That an immediate armistice be signed between Poland and
Soviet Russia whereby hostilities shall be suspended; the terms
of this armistice should provide on the one hand that the Polish
Army shall immediately withdraw to the line provisionally laid
down last year by the Peace Conference as the eastern boundary
within which Poland was entitled to establish a Polish administration. This line runs approximately as follows: Grodno, Yalovka,
Nemirov, Brest-Litovsk, Dorogusk, Ustilug, east of Grubeshov,
Krylov, and thence west of Rava-Ruska, east of Przemysl to the
Carpathians. North of Grodno the line which will be held by the
Lithuanians will run along the railway line running from Grodno
to Vilna and thence to Dvinsk. On the other hand the armistice
should provide that the armies of Soviet Russia should stand at a
distance of 50 kilometres to the east of this line. In Eastern
Galicia each army will stand on the line which they occupy at the
date of the signature of the armistice". (*Cf.* Maps Nos. III, IV
and VI.)

Continuing, the Note implies that the line is to be regarded as an
approximate ethnographic frontier—the dividing line between
'Russian soil' and Poland's 'own territory':

* The American attitude to the question of Russia's boundaries was clearly
stated by U.S. Secretary Colby in his Note of 10 August 1920: "To summarize
the position of this Government, I would say . . . that it would regard with
satisfaction a declaration by the Allied and Associated Powers, that the territorial integrity and true boundaries of Russia shall be respected. These boundaries should properly include the whole of the former Russian Empire, with
the exception of Finland proper, ethnic Poland, and such territory as may by
agreement form a part of the Armenian State."

". . . While the British Government has bound itself to give no assistance to Poland for any purpose hostile to Russia and to take no action itself hostile to Russia, it is also bound under the Covenant of the League of Nations to defend the integrity and independence of Poland within its legitimate ethnographic frontiers. If, therefore, Soviet Russia, despite its repeated declarations accepting the independence of Poland, will not be content with the withdrawal of the Polish Armies from Russian soil on the condition of a mutual armistice, but intends to take action hostile to Poland in its own territory, the British Government and its Allies would feel bound to assist the Polish nation to defend its existence with all the means at their disposal".

The Note also contained a proposal for a Peace Conference to be held in London and "to be attended by representatives of Soviet Russia, Poland, Lithuania, Latvia and Finland, with the object of negotiating a final peace between Russia and its neighbouring States". Representatives of Eastern Galicia were "to state their case" at the Conference. As a separate proposal, the Note suggested that "an armistice should be similarly signed between the forces of Soviet Russia and General Wrangel", who should likewise be invited to London to discuss the future of his troops and refugees, though "not as a member of the Conference."

Mr. Chicherin's caustic reply to this Note was given on 18 July (see Section 28).*

* The immediate reaction—a week after the publication of the Note—on the proposed demarcation line of the distinguished Russian historian, Professor Paul Milyukov, who has been Foreign Minister in the Russian Provisional Government and responsible for the first proclamation of the independence of Poland in March 1917 (see Section 26), is of considerable historical interest:

"A casual glance at the ethnographical map will suffice to show that, should the Poles retire to these frontiers ascribed to them in December 1919, they would not remain within the ethnographical limits strictly speaking. The frontier suggested by the Conference closely approaches the ethnographical borders of Poland but goes somewhat east of them and leaves a certain margin for further more detailed delimitation. A withdrawal to these borders, however, signifies the renunciation by Poland of territories inhabited by a non-Polish population. The same principle is maintained further south with regard to Eastern Galicia, where the frontiers indicated by the Note correspond rather closely to the frontier already well-established between the Poles and the Ukrainians. Finally, with regard to the region north of Grodno, the Note rightly alludes to a 'line which will be held by the Lithuanians'. All this is but a return to elementary justice which had been trampled upon in favour of the Poles in order to carry out the crazy scheme of making Poland the bulwark of the Entente against Germany and against a weakened Russia".

APPENDIX 5

(Reference: Section 29)

1919—1920

Below are given Polish accounts (*a, b, c*) of the events of 1919–1920 and a brief outline of the Polish attitude of the question of frontiers with Russia.

(*a*) ". . . In May 1919 the Polish army had already occupied almost the entire country up to the present eastern frontier of Poland. It had been a comparatively easy victory, since the Soviets had not been able to throw all the weight of their forces against Poland, having at the same time to defend themselves against the Russian anti-bolshevik generals (Denikin, Yudenich and Kolchak).

"After having beaten the latter, the Soviets had to recover their breath. On the other hand, as they were afraid that the Polish advance might continue, Mr. Chicherin, on 22 December 1919, proposed to Poland, by means of a wireless message, to negotiate a peace. The Government of Warsaw left this rather too vague proposal unanswered.

"On 29 January 1920 Moscow sent a new note to Warsaw, this time signed by Lenin, President of the Council of the People's Commissars, Chicherin, Commissar for Foreign Affairs, and Trotski, War Commissar. This note solemnly assured Poland that the Soviet Republic 'had recognized and was recognizing officially and unreservedly the independence and the sovereignty of the Polish Republic'. It ended with a new request for peace negotiations. (On 23 February Mr. Rakovsky, in the name of the Soviet Republic of the Ukraine, adhered to the Russian proposal, and on 6 March he expressed the hope that Poland 'would no longer delay the opening of peace negotiations'.)

"On 4 February, Mr. Stanislaw Patek, Polish Minister for Foreign Affairs, informed Mr. Chicherin that his proposals would be considered and that an answer would be sent. The Government referred the question to the Commission for Foreign Affairs and that of the Army, which were to sit together in order to consider the

64

problem in all its aspects. Poland, at the same time, sounded the opinion of Paris and London. The Quay d'Orsay advised against negotiating with the Soviets; the Foreign Office's reply was that Poland would know which was the wise course to take.

"On 27 March, Mr. Patek sent to Mr. Chicherin the final text of the preliminary conditions for peace, i.e.

(1) Annulment of the crime of the Partitions of Poland; dis-annexation of the part taken by Russia.

(2) Recognition of the states arisen out of Russia.

(3) Restitution of all possessions of the Polish State, according to the frontiers of 1772; indemnization for the losses suffered by the Poles in the war of 1914 and during the revolution of 1917:

(4) Ratification of the Treaty on the part of Russia.

(5) Poland to decide the fate of the territories situated to the west of the frontiers of 1772, in agreement with the wish of the populations to be expressed through a plebiscite.

"The note ended with the suggestion to begin peace negotiations on 10 April in Borisov, a small town not far from the front line.

"It was answered the next day, 28 March, by Mr. Chicherin. He asked for 'the immediate cessation of hostilities over the whole front' and suggested that the negotiations should be carried out in 'one of the Esthonian towns'.

"On 1 April, Mr. Patek informed Moscow that the Polish Government could not accept the proposed armistice for the whole of the front, that it insisted in demanding that the conference should take place at Borisov and that it promised to suspend war activities in that sector for the time of the negotiations.

"On 8 April, Mr. Chicherin, annoyed, appealed to the Allied Powers by radio and informed them that 'the Soviets are faced with the unpleasant prospect of seeing the negotiations with Poland fall through over the question of a meeting place—a case without precedent in the history of international relations'.

"If the Soviets had sincerely desired peace, the 'question of a meeting place' would not have caused the failure of peace negotiations. This attitude therefore allows us to doubt the sincerity of their offer.

"The Soviet proposals provoked innumerable comments in the Polish press.

"As three centuries before [see Appendix No. 1, (a)—quotation

E

from the same source], Polish policy found itself at the cross roads. Two different policies resulted. One—realistic—wanted simply peace with Russia, without concern for the other states, more or less capable of independent existence, which had 'arisen out of Russia'. It wished to *incorporate* within the Polish State a part of the eastern boundary which had belonged to it before 1772, leaving the rest to Russia. The aim of this policy, especially advocated by the National Democrats, headed by Dmowski, was a National State.

"The other policy, idealistic and bold, based itself on the glorious traditions of the Union of Poland and Lithuania. It did not desire to *incorporate* but to *federalize*. The upholder of this principle was Pilsudski. In entering Vilna on 20 April 1919, he issued a proclamation to 'the people of the Grand Duchy of Lithuania' which was inspired by his idea of a federation. The Marshal applied the same policy to the south-east. Like the National-Democrats, he too wanted peace in the east, but, from the military point of view, he did not think that the time had come for negotiations, and, from the political point of view, he wanted first to free the Ukraine. . . .

"On 26 April the Polish armies, commanded by General Pilsudski in person, launched a sudden offensive, together with the Ukrainian troops of Petlura. The Red armies were routed and a huge booty fell into the hands of the Poles, who on 7 May 1920 entered Kiev."

(From Casimir Smogorzewski's book *La Pologne Restaurée*, Gebethner & Wolff, Paris, 1927, pp. 141–143, 146.)

(b) Professor Stanislaw Grabski, who was at the time Chairman of the Foreign Affairs Committee of the Polish Diet and member of the Polish Peace Delegation at Riga, explains in his book *The Polish-Soviet Frontier* (London, 1943) why the majority of his Committee was decidedly in favour of Pilsudski's scheme. "This was not, after all, surprising", he says, "for both sentimental considerations and the loftiest traditions of the Polish struggle—'for our freedom and yours'—favoured a programme which proposed to liberate from Russian rule, no matter whether Tsarist or Bolshevik, all the districts torn from the Polish Republic in 1772, 1793, and 1795 and to give their populations full freedom to decide concerning their own political future. Further, the whole left wing were certain, and the majority of the centre confidently hoped, that if Poland by armed force aided the Ukraine and White Ruthenia to gain their political independence, they would, in gratitude, voluntarily enter such a union with Poland as existed at the end of the fourteenth century, or at least make a permanent, close alliance with it. Accordingly Pilsudski's programme was widely known among the Polish public as the federative or Jagellonian programme. . . ." (p. 20.)

". . . When, despite the assurances of Petlura and Makhno of a coming nationalist uprising in the Ukraine, the thirty million population furnished less than forty thousand sabres to fight for its independence, Pilsudski concluded that he must relinquish his federal programme; for it would be impossible to set up national Ukrainian and White Ruthenian States by Polish armed force when the great majority of the population showed no patriotic feeling." (p. 28.)

(c) According to Stanislaw Mackiewicz (*Colonel Beck and his policy*, Eyre & Spottiswoode, London, 1944, p. 77)—"During the bolshevik war of 1919–20 Russia was so weak as to be almost non-existent. Nobody knew whether there would be a bolshevik dictatorship, a return to constitutional monarchy or a break-up of Russia into its component countries. Pilsudski favoured the latter alternative. He visualized Poland, as strong as possible, associated with a Ukraine governed from Kiev and supported in turn by a free Caucasus. Poland would thus be at the head of a long chain of anti-Russian nations, spreading from the Gulf of Finland, from Tallinn, to the Caspian, Tiflis, and Baku."

* * *

The federative or Jagellonian programme of Pilsudski and his socialist group had met with opposition already at the time of the Paris Peace Conference, when the Polish delegates argued against Pilsudski's policy of 'liberation.' Roman Dmowski and Erasme Piltz had even feared that should Lithuania and Ukraine acquire independence, "Poland would ultimately be strangled and submerged". (D. H. Miller, *My Diary at the Conference of Peace*. Vol. XIV. p. 61. Summary of Mr. Dmowski's address to the Conference on 29 January 1919.) Mr. Dmowski, with the majority of his colleagues at the Conference (Piltz, Kosicki, Bertoszewicz, Seyda and others), opposed Pilsudski's idea of a federation embracing all historical Polish lands also on the grounds that "a federation under existing conditions would mean weakness and paralysis—we, instead, wish for a strong and united Poland, with a majority of Polish population". (Casimir Smogorzewski, *La Pologne Restaurée*. Paris, 1927, p. 155.)

Indeed, according to data on Polish population (estimates published in 1916 by Erasme Piltz in *Petite Encyclopédie Polonaise* pp. 11–12) the number of Poles in the Kingdom of Poland (Russian Poland), Lithuania, White Russia and Ukraine (Volhynia, Podolia and Kiev provinces) taken together, would amount *to less than one-third* of the total population, and in the last three regions *to less than one-tenth*. The individual percentages were as follows: in the Kingdom of Poland, 74·0 per cent of Poles—in the Provinces of Vilna, 26·5 per cent; Kovno, 11·4; Grodno, 17·0—Minsk, 10·3; Vitebsk, 8·6; Moghilev, 3·0—Volhynia, 9·9; Podolia, 8·7; Kiev, 2·9.

However, even within the boundaries claimed by Mr. Dmowski in 1919, the Poles would hardly have represented a majority. At the Paris Peace Conference his demands, as is known, were not found acceptable. "When the Poles presented their case to the Conference", wrote Mr. Lloyd George (*The Truth about the Peace Treaties*, Gollancz, 1938, p. 972), "their claims were by every canon of self-determination extravagant and inadmissible."*

---

* "Great Britain was the only Power which found herself in the unhappy position of opposing or seeking to limit the Polish claims in all the main questions where there were substantial differences of opinion. The wisdom or unwisdom of the British attitude can be judged only by history, but it is necessary to insist that this attitude arose from no unfriendliness towards Poland. It arose from a deeply rooted belief that if Poland was to be strong both internally and externally it was necessary that self-determination should be the guiding principle of the settlement".

If besides the inevitable Jewish and German minorities "Poland were to receive in the west more than the necessary minimum of Germans and in the east quantities of unwilling Lithuanians, White Russians, and Ruthenians her political effectiveness would decrease with the increase of her size, and she would become, like the former Austrian Empire, a conglomerate of nationalities incapable of securing even-handed justice and of working a democratic form of Government. Externally she would be surrounded by a ring of enemies, smarting under a sense of injustice, preaching a gospel of irredentism, fostering faction within her borders, and waiting an opportunity—which would not be difficult to find—for military aggression. And these enemies would be two of the greatest Powers of Europe—Russia and Germany".

(Professor Temperley's *History of the Peace Conference of Paris*. Vol. VI, 1924, pp. 239, 240.)

Differences between the French and British points of view on the future

Our Map No. VI is a reproduction of the map presented by Mr. Dmowski to the Peace Conference. The statistical data on which it is based is at variance with Mr. Piltz's data published in 1916, and with Mr. Dmowski's data of 1909 (*Cf.* Map No. III) and 1917 (*Cf.* Mr. Dmowski's Memorandum presented to Mr. Balfour in March 1917): in the case of the Vilna province, for instance, the 1919 map shows a Polish *majority*, whereas Mr. Piltz (in 1916) claimed for the Poles only 26·5 per cent, and Mr. Dmowski (in 1917), 35 per cent.†

*　　　　*　　　　*

"The Russians, whose interests were affected at many . . . points, suffered from having no representatives who could speak for the country as a whole. With the Bolsheviks the Conference had no

boundaries of Poland had existed already at the time of the Armistice:

"On 1 November 1919, M. Clemenceau raised the question of the evacuation of Poland by the German troops. On the 2nd, Marshal Foch proposed a draft-clause requiring the evacuation 'of all Polish territories, including those of Old Poland, that is, pre-partition Poland'. M. Pichon supported Foch, emphasizing that they had in mind 'Poland prior to the first partition of 1772'. This suggestion alarmed Mr. Balfour, who said: 'It is not this that we undertook; we undertook to reconstitute a Poland composed of Poles'."

(Casimir Smogorzewski, *op. cit.*, p. 139, quoting M. Mermeix, *Les Négociations Secrètes et les Quatre Armistices*. Paris, 1920.)

French policy in regard to Poland during the Peace Conference is thus described by André Tardieu: "For six months France has been carrying on a struggle on behalf of Poland against British prejudice—struggling for Danzig, Upper Silesia, Lvov, for the transport of Haller's divisions, struggling for war supplies, for the blockade of the Baltic, for the fulfilment of our obligations in December 1919, for the Statute of Eastern Galicia."

(André Tardieu, *La Paix*, Payot & Co., Paris, 1921, p. 427.)

† "The only fairly reliable figures of population [for the Province of Vilna and the City of Vilna] were those of the Russian census of 1897. These were necessarily out-of-date but seemed free from bias. Subsequent attempts at enumeration (Russian, German and Polish) were all incomplete and were also made in order to support particular theses.

The 1897 figures gave the following approximate percentages:

For the Province of Vilna including the City

Russians	White Russians	Poles	Lithuanians	Jews	Others
5·00	56·05	8·18	17·59	12·72	0·46

For the City of Vilna

20·50	4·20	30·90	2·00	40·30	2·10"

(*Survey of International Affairs*, 1920–1923, by Professor Arnold A. Toynbee. Published under the auspices of the British Institute of International Affairs, Oxford University Press, 1927, pp. 255–6.)

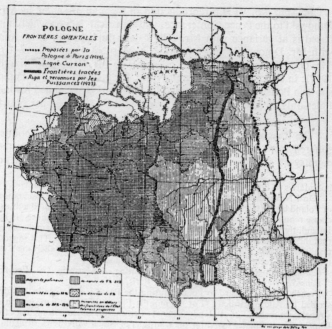

CARTE ETHNOGRAPHIQUE DE LA POLOGNE
(jointe à la note du 3 mars 1919 et sur laquelle nous avons
marqué la frontière de Riga).

MAP VIA.

Polish map submitted to the Paris Peace Conference in March,
1919 (to which have been added the Curzon Line and Riga Frontier).

Reproduced by kind permission of Mr. Casimir Smogorzewski from
his book *La Pologne Restaurée*, Gebethner & Wolff, Paris, 1927

official dealings, while the other Russian representatives had behind
them only portions of the former Russian Empire, and, being un-
recognized, were unable to put forward authoritative claims. As a
consequence the case of the Russians was inadequately expressed

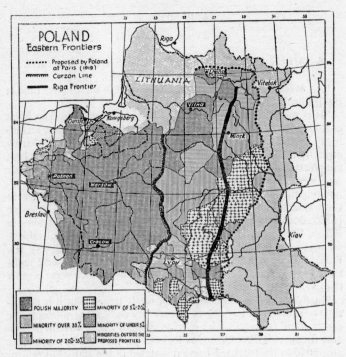

POLAND
Eastern Frontiers

······· Proposed by Poland
        at Paris (1919)
︿︿︿︿ Curzon Line
━━━━ Riga Frontier

POLISH MAJORITY

MINORITY OVER 33%

MINORITY OF 20%-35%

MINORITY OF 5%-20%

MINORITY OF UNDER 5%

MINORITIES OUTSIDE THE
PROPOSED FRONTIERS

MAP VIB. Redrawing of Map VIA.
For the distribution of Polish population see page 69.

and imperfectly appreciated. Their general position was that they
accepted the independence of Poland within her ethnographic limits,
but disputed all claims to territory farther east". " . . . The relations
of the Great Powers with the Bolsheviks not only deprived the
Russians of adequate opportunities for stating their case, but also
secured for the Poles a degree of consideration which they would not
have received if Russia had still been regarded as an ally".

(Professor Temperley's *History of the Peace Conference of Paris*,
published under the auspices of the British Institute of International Affairs, O.U. Press, 1924, Vol. VI, pp. 237 & 242.)

APPENDIX 6

(*Reference: Section* 29)

NUMBER OF POLES EAST OF THE CURZON LINE

". . . What number of Poles were there east of the Curzon Line at the [Polish] census of 1931?

"It is not possible to give a fully satisfactory answer. The Poles extended the province of Lvov far west of the Curzon Line, including in it West Galician territory with about 800,000 Poles and hardly any Ukrainians, thus obliterating the ethnic border between East and West Galicia. Further, of the Ukrainians in East Galicia, 60 per cent were entered as speaking 'Ukrainian', while 40 per cent inhabiting the same districts and differing in no way from the others in their speech, were registered as speaking the 'Ruski' language (which does not mean Russian, for which there is a different name in Polish, 'Rosyjski', and a separate column in the statistical tables). Or again, in the province of Polesie, where there were very few Poles, two-thirds of the population, 707,000 in number, were registered as speaking the 'local' (tutejszy) language, which was no other than White Russian.

"Such sources of confusion can be easily traced. But it is impossible to check with any degree of accuracy misleading entries in the census itself. In certain cases religion supplies a corrective to nationality figures: a Greek Orthodox Russian peasant will be much more amenable to his language being mis-stated in the statistical returns than to any tampering with his religion. Less reliable is the same criterion in the case of the Greek Catholics. With them 'occasional conformity' was by no means rare, and may account for statistical deviations. Worst of all is the case of the Roman Catholic White Russians, one of the most primitive peoples in Europe: Roman Catholicism was known in Western Russia as the 'Polish faith', and White Russians would in that sense let themselves be described as 'Poles'.

"At the census of 1931 there were in East Galicia nearly 1,600,000 Roman Catholics, over 3,000,000 Greek Catholics, and about 550,000 Jews. It is, to say the least, remarkable that between 1911 and 1931 the Roman Catholics in East Galicia should have increased by more than a third, while the number of Greek Catholics seems to

72

have suffered a slight decline. Roman Catholics and Greek Catholics live intermixed in the same districts and even in the same communes were affected more or less in the same way by war or emigration while the natural increase was, if anything, greater among the Greek Catholics. There was, no doubt, an influx of Polish officials and a certain number of officially assisted settlers to East Galicia between 1919 and 1939. Still, the growth in the number of Roman Catholics and the absence of increase in that of the Greek Catholics can only be explained by wrong entries or 'conversions' of a political and social character—it was often advantageous to Greek Catholics seeking employment with the State, or at Polish manor houses, to declare themselves Roman Catholics. If the total of genuine and autochthonous Poles in East Galicia is placed at 1,250,000, the figure will hardly prove an under-estimate.

"The population of the northern provinces east of the Curzon Line (Vilna, Novogrodek, Polesie, Volhynia, and the easternmost part of Bialystok) comprised in 1931 almost 1,800,000 Roman Catholics, 3,500,000 Greek Orthodox and about 550,000 Jews. The Greek Orthodox were either Ukrainians or White Russians. Of the Roman Catholics probably almost 200,000 were Lithuanians, Germans, Czechs, etc., and if the number who have to be booked as White Russians are placed somewhere halfway between the Russian over-estimate of 1931 we obtain for them the figure of 500,000–600,000. Lastly, here, too, in certain districts a remarkable increase can be noticed in the numbers of Roman Catholics, probably due to an importation of officials and settlers. The number of genuine, autochthonous Poles in these northern provinces will not have been very much more than 1,000,000.

"Thus, on a liberal estimate, there were hardly more than 2,250,000 to 2,500,000 Poles east of the Curzon Line, in a total population of over 11,000,000".

('The Russian-Polish Frontier', Special Article, *The Times*, 12 January 1944.)

* * *

Below the reader will find a Polish estimate on the population between the Curzon Line and the Frontier of Riga. The calculation is based on the figures for languages of 1931 Polish census. ('Poland and Russia—disputed area in figures' by C. Smogorzewski, *Free*

Europe, 21 April 1944.) No *official* Polish estimate for this area has been published.

Total Population (1931)	10,768,000
Poles	3,914,000 (36.4%)
Ukrainians	4,365,000 (40.6%)
White-Ruthenians	1,284,000 (11.8%)
Russians	102,000 (0.9%)
Lithuanians	76,000 (0.7%)
Jews*	899,000 (8.4%)
Others†	128,000 (1.2%)

No similar calculation for this area, based on Russian and Austrian statistics, is available.

* [According to another Polish source (Cz. Poznanski)—"of the 3,000,000 Jews who lived in Poland before the war, over one half lived in the area east of the Curzon Line".—EDITOR'S NOTE.]

† [In other estimates this group includes, in addition to the 128,000, some three-quarters of a million Polesians, who described themselves as speaking the 'local language'.—EDITOR'S NOTE.]

APPENDIX 7

(*Reference: Section* 34)

DOCUMENTS

Some of the official statements (taken from *The Times, Soviet War News* and *Free Europe*) in April–May 1943 and January–February 1944.

Extract from the Statement by the Soviet Information Bureau on the Katyn murder German accusation, 15 *April* 1943.

In the past two or three days Goebbels' slanderers have been spreading vile fabrications alleging that Soviet authorities effected a mass shooting of Polish officers in the spring of 1940, in the Smolensk area. In launching this monstrous invention the German-Fascist scoundrels do not hesitate at the most unscrupulous and base lies, in their attempt to cover up crimes which, as has now become evident, were perpetrated by themselves.

The German-Fascist reports on this subject leave no doubt as to the tragic fate of the former Polish prisoners of war who in 1941 were engaged in construction work in areas west of Smolensk and who, along with many Soviet people, residents of the Smolensk region, fell into the hands of the German-Fascist hangmen in the summer of 1941, after the withdrawal of the Soviet troops from this area. . . .

Extract from the Statement by the Polish Minister of National Defence, General Marjan Kukiel, 16 *April* 1943.

On 17 September 1940 the official organ of the Red Army, *Krasnaja Zvezda*, reported that during the fighting after 17 September 1939, 181,000 Polish prisoners of war had been taken by the Soviets, among them about 10,000 Polish officers and reserve officers. According to information in the possession of the Polish Government, three large prisoner-of-war camps were set up on Soviet territory in November 1939 at Kozelsk (to the east of Smolensk), Starobelsk, near Kharkov, and Ostaskov, near Kalinin; in the latter police and military police were held.

At the beginning of 1940 the camp authorities informed the prisoners in all three camps that the camps would be closed shortly and that they would be able to return to their families. Lists were made allegedly for this purpose stating exactly where the various prisoners wished to go on their release. At the same time there were :

(1) Kozelsk Camp: 5,000 prisoners, among them 4,500 officers ;

(2) Starobelsk Camp: 3,920 prisoners, 100 of them civilians, the rest officers, among them nearly 400 medical officers ;

(3) Ostaskov Camp: 6,570 prisoners, among them 380 officers.

On 5 April 1940 the Soviet authorities started to empty the camps, groups of 60 to 300 men being removed every few days up to the middle of May. From Kozelsk they were deported in the direction of Smolensk. Only about 400 persons in all from all three camps were deported in June 1940 to Griazovets, in the Vologda province. . . .

At the end of August 1941 a group of Polish officers from Griazovets arrived at Buzuluk where the Polish units were, but not one of the officers deported in a different direction from Kozelsk, Starobelsk, and Ostaskov appeared there. In all, therefore, about 8,300 officers were missing apart from the 7,000 others, such as N.C.O.'s, soldiers, and civilians, who were in those camps at the time of their liquidation.

Ambassador Kot and General Anders concerned at this state of affairs, approached the Soviet authorities to intervene and make inquiries about the fate of the Polish officers from the camps. . . .

On 3 December 1941 General Sikorski during his visit to Moscow also intervened. In a conversation with Premier Stalin he produced an incomplete list containing the names of 3,843 Polish officers made out by the fellow-prisoners. Premier Stalin assured General Sikorski that the amnesty was of a general nature and affected both military and civilian persons and that the Soviet Government had released all Polish officers. An additional list of 800 officers was handed to Premier Stalin by General Anders on 18 March 1942 but not one of the officers in those lists has been sent back to the Polish Army.

. . . On 28 January 1942 Minister Raczynski handed a Note on behalf of the Polish Government to the Ambassador, M. Bogomolov . . .

Ambassador Bogomolov informed Minister Raczynski, in a Note dated 13 March 1942 that in accordance with the decree issued by the

Executive of the Supreme Council of the U.S.S.R. on 12 August 1941, and with the Declarations by the People's Commissariat for Foreign Affairs on 8 and 19 November 1941, the amnesty had been carried out in full and applied to both military and civilian persons.

On 19 May 1942 Ambassador Kot sent to the People's Commissariat for Foreign Affairs a memorandum in which he expressed his regret at the refusal to provide the lists of the prisoners, and his concern as to their fate, thereby stressing the value those officers would have in the war operations against the Germans. On no occasion has the Polish Government or the Polish Embassy in Kujbysev ever received an answer as to the whereabouts of the officers and other prisoners deported from the three above-mentioned camps.

We have become accustomed to the lies of German propaganda and understand the purpose of its recent revelations, but in view of the detailed information given by the Germans concerning the finding of the bodies of many thousands of Polish officers near Smolensk and the categorical declaration that they were murdered by the Soviets in Spring 1940, the necessity has arisen that the mass graves which have been discovered should be investigated and the facts verified by a proper international body, such as the authorities of the International Red Cross. The Polish Government is approaching that institution with a view to their sending a delegation to the place in which the Polish prisoners of war are said to have been massacred.

Statement by the Polish Government, 17 April 1943.

There is no Pole who would not be deeply shocked by the news of the discovery near Smolensk in a common grave of massacred bodies of the Polish officers missing in the U.S.S.R. and of the mass execution of which they have become victims, news of which is being given the widest publicity by German propaganda. The Polish Government on 15 April instructed their representative in Switzerland to request the International Red Cross in Geneva to send a delegation which would investigate on the spot the true state of affairs. It is to be desired that the findings of this protecting institution which is to be entrusted with the task of clarifying the matter and of establishing responsibility, should be issued without any delay.

At the same time, however, the Polish Government, on behalf of the Polish nation, denies to the Germans the right to draw from a crime which they ascribe to others arguments in their own defence.

77

The profoundly hypocritical indignation of the German propaganda will not succeed in concealing from the world the many cruel, repeated, and still lasting crimes committed on the Polish people.

The Polish Government recalls such facts as:

The removal of Polish officers from prisoner-of-war camps in the Reich and the subsequent shooting of them for political offences alleged to have been committed before the war.

Mass arrests of reserve officers subsequently deported to concentration camps, to die a slow death (from Cracow and the neighbouring district alone 6,000 were deported in June 1942).

The compulsory enlistment into the German Army of Polish war prisoners from territories illegally incorporated into the Reich.

The forcible conscription of about 200,000 Poles from the same territories, and the execution of the families of those who managed to escape.

The massacre of one-and-a-half million people by executions and in concentration camps.

The recent imprisonment of 80,000 people of military age, officers and men, and the torturing and murdering of them in the camps of Majdanek and Tremblinka.

It is not to enable the Germans to lay impudent claims to appear in the role of defenders of Christianity and the European civilization that Poland is making immense sacrifices and fighting and enduring immeasurable sufferings. The blood of Polish soldiers and Polish citizens, wherever shed, cries for expiation before the conscience of the free peoples of the world. The Polish Government deny the right to exploit all the crimes committed against Polish citizens for political manœuvres by whoever is guilty of these crimes.

Soviet Government's Note on the severance of diplomatic relations with the Polish Government in London, 26 April 1943.

The recent attitude of the Polish Government in respect of the U.S.S.R. is regarded as absolutely abnormal by the Soviet Government, and as disregarding all rules and normal procedure governing the relationship of two allied countries.

The campaign, hostile to the Soviet Government, started by the German Fascists concerning the Polish officers murdered by them in the area of Smolensk in the territory occupied by the Germans, was immediately seized upon by the Polish Government and in every way enlarged upon by the Polish official Press. Not only have the

Polish Government failed to administer a rebuff to the perfidious Fascist calumny against the U.S.S.R., but they have not even deemed it necessary to address inquiries or requests for explanation to the Soviet Government in that connection.

The Hitlerite authorities, having committed an appalling crime in respect of the Polish officers, now stage a farcical investigation, and for the staging of this they have made use of several Polish pro-Fascist elements, specially selected by them from occupied Poland, where everybody is under Hitler's heel and where no honest Pole dares to express himself honestly and freely. For the 'investigation', both the Polish Government and the Hitlerite Government invited the International Red Cross, which is compelled in the conditions of the terroristic regime, with its gallows and mass extermination of the peaceful population, to take part in this investigation farce staged by Hitler. Clearly such 'investigation', conducted behind the back of the Soviet Government, cannot evoke the confidence of honest people.

The fact that the hostile campaign against the Soviet Union was launched simultaneously by the German and Polish Press, and is conducted in the same spirit, leaves no doubt that between the enemy of the allies, Hitler and the Polish Government there is contact and agreement for the prosecution of this campaign. While the people of the Soviet Union, shedding blood in the hard struggle against Hitlerite Germany, are exerting all their power for the defeat of the common enemy of the Russian and Polish people and of all the freedom-loving democratic nations, the Polish Government, in deference to Hitler's tyranny, deals a treacherous blow against the Soviet Union.

The Soviet Government are aware that this hostile campaign against the Soviet Union has been launched by the Polish Government for the purpose of utilizing Hitler's calumnious lie in order to exercise pressure on the Soviet Government for the purpose of obtaining from them territorial concessions at the expense of the interests of the Soviet Ukraine, White Russia, and Soviet Lithuania. All these circumstances force the Soviet Government to take the view that the present Polish Government, who have taken the path of accord with Hitler's Government, have, indeed, discontinued the relations of alliance with the Soviet Union, and have assumed a position hostile to the Soviet Union. In view of the foregoing, the Soviet Government have decided to sever relations with the Polish Government.

Polish reply of 29 *April* 1943 *to the Soviet Note of* 26 *April* 1943.

The Polish Government affirm that their policy aiming at a friendly understanding between Poland and Soviet Russia on the basis of the integrity and full sovereignty of the Polish Republic was and continues to be fully supported by the Polish nation.

Conscious of their responsibility towards their own nation and towards the allies, whose unity and solidarity the Polish Government consider to be the corner-stone of future victory, they were the first to approach the Soviet Government with a proposal for a common understanding, in spite of the many tragic events which had taken place from the moment of the entry of the Soviet Armies on the territory of the Republic, i.e. 17 September 1939.

Having regulated their relations with Soviet Russia by the Agreement of 30 July 1941 and by the understanding of 4 December 1941, the Polish Government have scrupulously discharged their obligations.

Acting in close union with their Government, the Polish people, making the extreme sacrifice, fight implacably in Poland and outside the frontiers of their country against the German invader. No traitor quisling has sprung from the Polish ranks. All collaboration with the Germans has been scorned. In the light of facts known throughout the world, the Polish Government and Polish nation have no need to defend themselves from any suggestion of contact or understanding with Hitler.

In a public statement of 17 April 1943 the Polish Government categorically denied to Germany the right to abuse the tragedy of Polish officers for her own perfidious schemes. They unhesitatingly denounce Nazi propaganda designed to create mistrust between allies. About the same time a Note was sent to the Soviet Ambassador accredited to the Polish Government asking once again for information which would help to elucidate the fate of the missing officers.

The Polish Government and people look to the future. They appeal in the name of the solidarity of the United Nations and elementary humanity for the release from the U.S.S.R. of the thousands of the families of Polish armed forces engaged in the fight or preparing in Great Britain and the Middle East to take their part in the fight—tens of thousands of Polish orphans and children for the education of whom they would take full responsibility and who now, in view of the German mass slaughter, are particularly precious to the Polish people. The Polish Army, in waging the war against Germany, will also require for reinforcement all fighting Polish males who are now on Soviet soil, and the Polish Government appeal for their release. They reserve their right to plead the cause of all these persons to the world. In conclusion the Polish Government ask for the continuation of relief welfare for the mass of Polish citizens who will remain in the U.S.S.R.

In defending the integrity of the Polish Republic, which accepted the war with the Third Reich, the Polish Government never claimed, and do not claim, in accordance with their statement of 25 February 1943 any Soviet territories. It is, and will be, the duty of every Polish Government to defend the rights of Poland and of Polish citizens. The principles for which the United Nations are fighting, and also the making of all efforts for strengthening their solidarity in this struggle against the common enemy, remain the unchanging basis of the policy of the Polish Government.

Marshal Stalin's Statement, 3 *May* 1943.
Reply to questions put to Marshal Stalin by the London Times *and* New York Times *in Moscow on Soviet-Polish relations.*

On 3 May I received your two questions concerning Polish-Soviet relations. Here are my answers:

QUESTION 1: Does the Government of the U.S.S.R. desire to see a strong and independent Poland after the defeat of Hitlerite Germany?

ANSWER: Unquestionably, it does.

QUESTION 2: On what fundamentals is it your opinion that relations between Poland and the U.S.S.R. should be based after the war?

ANSWER: Upon the fundamentals of solid good neighbourly relations and mutual respect, or, should the Polish people so desire, upon the fundamentals of alliance providing for mutual assistance against the Germans as the chief enemies of the Soviet Union and Poland.

[See also a statement on Polish-Soviet relations (1941–43) made by A. Y. Vyshinski, Assistant People's Commissar of Foreign Affairs (6 May 1943; full text in *Soviet War News*, No. 556) and a reply by Count Edward Raczynski, Polish Foreign Minister (7 May 1943; in *Free Europe*, 21 May 1943).]

Conclusions of the Special Commission investigating the circumstances of the shooting of Polish prisoners by the Germans in the Katyn Forest.

This Report was published in January 1944 and the full text in English appeared in a special supplement to *Soviet War News.*

"From all the material at the disposal of the Special Commission, namely evidence given by over 100 witnesses questioned, data supplied by the medico-legal experts, documents and material evidence found in the graves in the Katyn Forest, the following conclusions emerge with irrefutable clarity:

(1) The Polish prisoners of war who were in the three camps west of Smolensk, and employed on road building before the outbreak of war, remained there after the German invaders reached Smolensk, until September 1941, inclusive.

(2) In the Katyn Forest, in the autumn of 1941, the German occupation authorities carried out mass shootings of Polish prisoners of war from the above-named camps.

(3) The mass shootings of Polish prisoners of war in the Katyn Forest was carried out by a German military organisation hiding behind the conventional name 'H.Q. of the 537th Engineering Battalion', which consisted of Ober-leutnant Arnes, his assistant Ober-leutnant Rekst, and Lieutenant Hott.

(4) In connection with the deterioration of the general military and political situation for Germany at the beginning of the year 1943, the German occupation authorities, with provocational aims, took a number of steps in order to ascribe their own crimes to the organs of the Soviet Power, calculating on setting Russians and Poles at loggerheads.

(5) With this aim, (*a*) the German-Fascist invaders, using persuasion, attempts at bribery, threats and barbarous torture, tried to find witnesses among Soviet citizens, from whom they tried to extort false evidence alleging that the Polish prisoners of war had been shot by the organs of Soviet Power in the spring of 1940; (*b*) the German occupation authorities in the spring of 1943 brought in from other districts bodies of Polish war prisoners whom they had shot and put them into the open graves in the Katyn Forest, calculating on covering up the traces of their own crimes, and on increasing the number of 'victims of Bolshevik atrocities' in the Katyn Forest; (*c*) preparing for their provocation, the German occupation authorities started opening the graves in the Katyn Forest, in order

to take out documents and material evidence which exposed them, using for this work about 500 Russian prisoners of war who were shot by the Germans after the work was completed.

(6) It has been established beyond doubt from the evidence of the medico-legal experts, that (*a*) the time of the shooting was the autumn of 1941; (*b*) in shooting the Polish war prisoners the German hangmen applied the same method of pistol shots in the back of the head as they applied in the mass execution of Soviet citizens in other towns, e.g. Orel, Voronezh, Krasnodar and Smolensk itself.

(7) The conclusions drawn from the evidence given by witnesses, and from the findings of the medico-legal experts on the shooting of Polish war prisoners by the Germans in the autumn of 1941, are completely confirmed by the material evidence and documents excavated from the Katyn graves.

(8) In shooting the Polish war prisoners in the Katyn Forest, the German-Fascist invaders consistently carried out their policy of physical extermination of the Slav peoples."

SIGNED:

Chairman of the Commission, Academician BURDENKO.

Members:

Academician ALEXEI TOLSTOY.

The Metropolitan NIKOLAI.

Chairman of the All-Slav Committee, Lieutenant-General GUNDOROV.

Chairman of the Executive Committee of the Union of the Red Cross and Red Crescent Societies, KOLESNIKOV.

People's Commissar for Education of the Russian S.F.S.R., Academician POTEMKIN.

Chief of the Central Medical Administration of the Red Army, Colonel-General SMIRNOV.

Chairman of the Smolensk Regional Executive Committee, MELNIKOV.

Smolensk, 24 *January* 1944.

Statement by the Polish Government, 5 January 1944.

In their victorious struggle against the German invader the Soviet forces are reported to have crossed the frontier of Poland. This fact is another proof of the breaking down of the German resistance and it foreshadows the inevitable military defeat of Germany.

It fills the Polish nation with the hope that the hour of liberation is drawing near. Poland was the first nation to take up the German challenge, and it has been fighting against the invaders for over four years at the cost of tremendous sacrifices and sufferings without producing a single quisling, and rejecting any form of compromise or collaboration with the aggressor.

The underground movement, among its many activities, concentrated upon attacking the Germans in their most sensitive spots, upon sabotage in every possible form, and on the carrying out of many death sentences on German officials whose conduct had been particularly outrageous.

The Polish forces, twice reorganized outside their country, have been fighting ceaselessly in the air, at sea and on land side by side with our allies, and there is no front on which Polish blood has not been mingled with the blood of other defenders of freedom.

There is no country in the world where Poles have not contributed to furthering the common cause. The Polish nation, therefore, is entitled to expect full justice and redress as soon as it is set free from enemy occupation. The first condition of such justice is the earliest re-establishment of Polish sovereign administration in the liberated territories of the Republic of Poland and the protection of life and property of Polish citizens.

The Polish Government as the only legal steward and spokesman of the Polish nation recognized by Poles at home and abroad, as well as by allied and free Governments, is conscious of the contribution of Poland to the war, and is responsible for the fate of the nation. It affirms its indestructible right to independence, confirmed by the principles of the Atlantic Charter, common to all the United Nations, and by binding international treaties. The provisions of those treaties, based on the free agreement of the parties, not on the enforcement of the will of one side to the detriment of the other, cannot be revised by accomplished facts.

The conduct of the Polish nation in the course of the present war has proved that it has never recognised, and will not recognise, solutions imposed by force. The Polish Government expects that the Soviet Union, sharing its views as to the importance of future friendly relations between the two countries in the interests of peace, and with a view to preventing German revenge, will not fail to respect the rights and interests of the Polish Republic and its citizens.

Acting in that belief, the Polish Government instructed the underground authorities in Poland on 27 October 1943 to continue and intensify their resistance to the German invaders, to avoid all conflicts with the Soviet armies entering Poland in their battle against the Germans, and to enter into co-operation with the Soviet commanders in the event of the resumption of Polish-Soviet relations.

If a Polish-Soviet agreement such as the Polish Government has declared itself willing to conclude had preceded the crossing of the frontier of Poland by the Soviet forces, such an agreement would have enabled the Polish underground army to co-ordinate its action against the Germans with the Soviet military authorities.

The Polish Government still considers such an arrangement highly desirable. At this crucial moment, the importance of which for the course of the war and for its outcome in Europe is evident to every one, the Polish Government issues the above declaration, confident in final victory and in the triumph of the just principles for which the United Nations stand.

[See also the broadcast speech of M. Mikolajczyk, Polish Prime Minister, on 7 January 1944.]

Statement by the Soviet Government, 11 *January* 1944.

A declaration of the *émigré* Polish Government in London on the question of Soviet-Polish relations was published on 5 January. It contains a number of incorrect assertions, including one about the Soviet-Polish frontier.

As is known, the Soviet constitution established the Soviet-Polish border in accordance with the will of the population of Western Ukraine and Western White Russia, expressed in a plebiscite which was carried out on a broad democratic basis in 1939. The territories of Western Ukraine, in which Ukrainians constitute the overwhelming majority of the population, were incorporated in Soviet Ukraine, and the territories of Western White Russia, in which White Russians constitute the overwhelming majority of the population, were incorporated in Soviet White Russia.

The injustice committed by the Riga Treaty of 1921, which was imposed upon the Soviet Union in regard to the Ukrainians inhabiting Western Ukraine, and the White Russians inhabiting western White Russia, was in this way rectified. The incorporation of Western Ukraine and Western White Russia in the Soviet Union not only did not violate the interests of Poland, but, on the contrary, created a reliable basis for a solid and permanent friendship between the Polish people and the neighbouring Ukrainian, White Russian, and Russian peoples.

The Soviet Government has repeatedly declared that it stands for the re-establishment of a strong and independent Poland and for friendship between the Soviet Union and Poland. The Soviet Government once again declares that it is seeking to establish friendship between the U.S.S.R. and Poland on the basis of solid good neighbourly relations and mutual respect, and—if the Polish people so desire—on the basis of an alliance of mutual assistance against the Germans as the main enemies of the Soviet Union and Poland. The realisation of this task could be served by Poland's joining the Soviet-Czechoslovak treaty of friendship, mutual assistance, and post-war collaboration.

The success of Soviet troops on the Soviet-German front every day hasten the liberation of the occupied territories of the Soviet Union from the German invaders. The self-sacrificing struggle of the Red Army and the developing military operations of our allies bring nearer the utter defeat of the Hitlerite war-machine and the liberation of Poland and other peoples from the yoke of the German invaders.

The 'Union of Polish Patriots in the U.S.S.R.' and the Polish army corps, formed by them, which is operating at the front against the Germans hand-in-hand with the Red Army, are already in this struggle for liberation. There opens up at present the possibility of the regeneration of Poland as a strong and independent State. But Poland must be reborn, not by means of the seizure of Ukrainian and White Russian lands, but through the restoration to Poland of lands which belonged to her from time immemorial and which were wrested from Poland by the Germans. Only in this way would it be possible to establish trust and friendship between the Polish, Ukrainian, White Russian and Russian peoples.

Poland's eastern frontiers can be established by agreement with the Soviet Union. The Soviet Government does not regard the 1939 frontiers as immutable. These frontiers can be modified in Poland's favour so that areas in which the Polish population forms the majority can be turned over to Poland.

In this case the Soviet-Polish frontier could pass approximately along the so-called Curzon Line, which was adopted in 1919 by the Supreme Council of Allied Powers and which provides for the inclusion of Western Ukraine and Western White Russia, in the Soviet Union.

Poland's western borders must be extended through the incorporation in Poland of ancient Polish land previously wrested by Germany and without which it is impossible to unite the whole Polish people in its State, which thereby will receive the necessary outlet to the Baltic Sea. The just aspirations of the Polish people for their reunion in a strong and independent State must receive recognition and support.

The *émigré* Polish Government, isolated from its people, has proved incapable of establishing friendly relations with the Soviet Union. It has also proved incapable of organizing an active struggle against the German invaders in Poland itself. Furthermore, by its incorrect policy it not infrequently plays into the hands of the German invaders.

However, the interests of Poland and the Soviet Union lie in the establishment of solid friendly relations between our countries, and in the people of Poland and the Soviet Union uniting in the struggle against the common external enemy, as is demanded by the common cause of all the allies.

The Polish reply of 15 January 1944 to the Soviet Statement of 11 January 1944.

(1) The Polish Government have taken cognizance of the declaration of the Soviet Government contained in the Tass communiqué of 11 January, which was issued as a reply to the declaration of the Polish Government of 5 January.

(2) The Soviet communiqué contains a number of statements to which a complete answer is afforded by the ceaseless struggle against the Germans waged at the heaviest cost by the Polish nation under the direction of the Polish Government. In their earnest anxiety to safeguard the complete solidarity of the United Nations, especially at a decisive stage of their struggle against the common enemy, the Polish Government consider it to be preferable now to refrain from further public discussions.

(3) While the Polish Government cannot recognize unilateral decisions or accomplished facts which have taken place or might take place on the territory of the Polish Republic, they have repeatedly expressed their sincere desire for a Polish-Soviet agreement on terms which would be just and acceptable to both sides.

(4) To this end the Polish Government are approaching the British and United States Governments with a view to securing through their intermediacy the discussion by the Polish and Soviet Governments, with the participation of the British and American Governments, of all outstanding questions, the settlement of which should lead to friendly and permanent co-operation between Poland and the Soviet Union. The Polish Government believes this to be desirable in the interest of the victory of the United Nations and harmonious relations in post-war Europe.

Statement by the Soviet Government, 17 *January* 1944.

(1) In the Polish declaration the main question of the recognition of the Curzon line as the Soviet-Polish frontier is entirely evaded and ignored, which can only be interpreted as a rejection of the Curzon line.

(2) As regards the Polish Government's proposal for the opening of official negotiations between it and the Soviet Government, the Soviet Government is of opinion that this proposal aims at misleading public opinion, for it is easy to understand that the Soviet Government is not in a position to enter into official negotiations with a Government with which diplomatic relations have been broken. Soviet circles wish that it should be borne in mind that diplomatic relations with the Polish Government were broken off through the fault of that Government because of its active participation in the hostile, anti-Soviet, slanderous campaign of the German invaders in connection with the alleged murders in Katyn.

(3) In the opinion of Soviet circles the above-mentioned circumstances once again demonstrate that the present Polish Government does not desire to establish good-neighbourly relations with the Soviet Union.

Extract from Mr. Churchill's speech in the House of Commons on 22 *February* 1944.

I took occasion to raise personally with Marshal Stalin the question of the future of Poland. I pointed out that it was in fulfilment of our guarantee to Poland that Great Britain declared war upon Nazi Germany and that we had never weakened in our resolve, even in the period when we were all alone, and that the fate of the Polish nation holds a prime place in the thoughts and policies of His Majesty's Government and of the British Parliament. It was with great pleasure that I heard from Marshal Stalin that he, too, was resolved upon the creation and maintenance of a strong, integral, independent Poland as one of the leading Powers in Europe. He has several times repeated these declarations in public and I am convinced that they represent the settled policy of the Soviet Union.

Here I may remind the House that we ourselves have never in the past guaranteed, on behalf of His Majesty's Government, any particular frontier line to Poland. We did not approve of the Polish occupation of Vilna in 1920. The British view in 1919 stands expressed in the so-called Curzon Line which attempted to deal, at any rate partially, with the problem. I have always held the opinion that all questions of territorial settlement and readjustment should stand over until the end of the war and that the victorious Powers should then arrive at formal and final agreements governing the articulation of Europe as a whole. That is still the view of His Majesty's Government. However, the advance of the Russian Armies into Polish regions in which the Polish underground is active makes it indispensable that some kind of friendly working agreement should be arrived at to govern the war-time conditions and to enable all anti-Hitlerite forces to work together with the greatest advantage against the common foe.

During the last few weeks the Foreign Secretary and I together have laboured with the Polish Government in London with the object of establishing a working arrangement upon which the Fighting Forces can act, and upon which I trust an increasing structure of goodwill and comradeship may be built between Russians and Poles. I have an intense sympathy with the Poles, that heroic race whose national spirit centuries of misfortune cannot quench, but I also have sympathy with the Russian standpoint. Twice in our lifetime Russia has been violently assaulted by Germany. Many millions of Russians have been slain and vast tracts of Russian soil devastated as a result of repeated German aggression. Russia has the right of reassurance against future attacks from the West, and we are going all the way with her to see that she gets it, not only by the might of her arms, but by the approval and assent of the United

Nations. The liberation of Poland may presently be achieved by the Russian armies after these armies have suffered millions of casualties in breaking the German military machine. I cannot feel that the Russian demand for a reassurance about her Western frontiers goes beyond the limit of what is reasonable or just. Marshal Stalin and I also spoke and agreed upon the need for Poland to obtain compensation at the expense of Germany both in the North and in the West. (*Hansard*, House of Commons, 22.2.1944: Cols. 697–8).